21
DAYS
BUILDING
HEALTHY
HABITS
FOR YOUR *family*

The quoted ideas expressed in this book (but not Scripture verses) are not, in all cases, exact quotations, as some have been edited for clarity and brevity. In all cases, the author has attempted to maintain the speaker's original intent. In some cases, quoted material for this book was obtained from secondary sources, primarily print media. While every effort was made to ensure the accuracy of these sources, the accuracy cannot be guaranteed. For additions, deletions, corrections, or clarifications in future editions of this text, please write Freeman-Smith, LLC.

Scripture quotations are taken from:

The Holy Bible, King James Version (KJV)

The Holy Bible, New King James Version (NKJV) Copyright © 1982 by Thomas Nelson, Inc. Used by permission.

The Holman Christian Standard Bible™ (HOLMAN CSB) Copyright © 1999, 2000, 2001 by Holman Bible Publishers. Used by permission.

Cover Design by Kim Russell / Wahoo Designs
Page Layout by Bart Dawson

ISBN 1-58334-314-8

Printed in the United States of America

Presented to:

_____

Date:

_____

21
DAYS
BUILDING
HEALTHY
HABITS.
FOR YOUR *family*

Table of Contents

Introduction

Maybe you've heard the old saying that it takes 21 days to change a habit. It's a common-sense idea that makes a valid point: if you can do anything for 21 straight days, then there's a very good chance you can keep doing it on the 22nd day, and the 23rd, and the 24th, and beyond.

If you thought that you and your family members could establish a number of healthy habits, would you be willing to carve out a few minutes each day for the next three weeks in order to find out? If you answered yes, congratulations! You and your loved ones are about to embark on a grand adventure.

This book contains 21 chapters, each of which contains a devotional message which addresses a healthy habit. If you and your family members read these devotionals together—and if you spend a few minutes talking about the things you've read—you might just make profound improvements in the collective life of your clan.

If your family is like most families, you've already tried, perhaps on many occasions, to form healthier habits. You've employed your own willpower in a noble effort to create new, improved lifestyles. Maybe you've gone on diets, or perhaps you've made New Year's resolutions, or perhaps you've tried other methods to finally make important changes in your lives. And if you're like most families, you've been successful . . . for a while. But eventually, those old familiar habits came creeping back, and the improvements that you had made proved to be temporary.

This book is intended to help you permanent make changes by working together as a family. In fact, at the end of each chapter, family members will be asked to "sign on" to the healthy habit of the day. If you and your loved ones work together—and if you all work in partnership with God—you're far more likely to make your new habits stick.

During the next 21 days, you and your family members will be asked to depend less upon your own willpower and more upon God's power as you focus on forming 21 life-altering habits. And make no mistake: when you and yours establish a working relationship with God, you'll be amazed by the things that can happen in 21 short days.

How to Use This Book

This text will be most effective if each chapter is read and discussed by all members of your family who are old enough to understand the concepts and contribute to the conversation. At the end of each chapter, you should jot down the changes that you and your loved ones intend to make in the section entitled "What We Can Do as a Family." Then, ask family members to "sign on" to those changes in the space provided at the end of each chapter.

If you and your loved ones can gather together for 21 straight days, so much the better. But if you can't seem to round everybody up at the same time, don't worry—you can still have individual discussions with each family member and ask him or her to "sign on" after you've thoroughly discussed each topic.

PART 1

Your Family's SPIRITUAL HEALTH

Nothing is more important than the condition of your family's spiritual health.

FORMING THE HABIT OF . . .

Obedience

Choose for yourselves today the one you will worship . . . . As for me and my family, we will worship the Lord.

Joshua 24:15 HOLMAN CSB

God has given us a guidebook for abundant life; that book is the Holy Bible. It contains thorough instructions which, if followed, lead to fulfillment, righteousness and salvation. But, if we choose to ignore God's commandments, the results are as predictable as they are tragic.

How can we demonstrate our love for God? By placing Christ squarely at the center of our lives. Jesus said that if we are to love Him, we must obey His commandments (John 14:15). Thus, our obedience to the Master is an expression of our love for Him.

In Ephesians 2:10 we read, "For we are His workmanship, created in Christ Jesus for good works" (NKJV). These words are instructive: We are not saved by good works, but for good works. Good works are not the root, but rather the fruit of our salvation.

> Obedience is the outward expression of your love of God.
>
> Henry Blackaby

When we seek righteousness in our own lives—and when we seek the companionship of those who do likewise—we reap the spiritual rewards that God intends for our lives. When we behave ourselves as godly people, we honor God. When we live righteously and according to God's commandments, He blesses us in ways that we cannot fully understand.

As families, we should take every step of our journey with God. We should continue to read His Word and we should continue to follow His commandments. We should support only those activities that further God's kingdom and our own spiritual growth. And we should be worthy examples to our friends and neighbors. When we do, we'll reap the blessings that God has promised to all those who live according to His will and His Word.

Believe and do what God says. The life-changing consequences will be limitless, and the results will be confidence and peace of mind.

Franklin Graham

God's love for His children is unconditional, no strings attached. But, God's blessings on our lives do come with a condition— obedience. If we are to receive the fullness of God's blessings, we must obey Him and keep His commandments.

Jim Gallery

We cannot rely on God's promises without obeying his commandments.

John Calvin

God uses ordinary people who are obedient to Him to do extraordinary things.

John Maxwell

Therefore, get your minds ready for action, being self-disciplined, and set your hope completely on the grace to be brought to you at the revelation of Jesus Christ. As obedient children, do not be conformed to the desires of your former ignorance but, as the One who called you is holy, you also are to be holy in all your conduct.

1 Peter 1:13-15 HOLMAN CSB

And the world with its lust is passing away, but the one who does God's will remains forever.

1 John 2:17 HOLMAN CSB

Now by this we know that we know Him, if we keep His commandments.

1 John 2:3 NKJV

But whoever keeps His word, truly the love of God is perfected in him. By this we know that we are in Him. He who says he abides in Him ought himself also to walk just as He walked.

1 John 2:5-6 NKJV

For More Thoughts About Obedience, Please Turn to Page 144

FAMILY VALUES

	CHECK ONE:	
	YES	NO

We will study God's Word.

We will strive to obey God's commandments.

We will associate with fellow believers who,
by their words and actions, encourage us
to obey God.

We will not willingly put ourselves in situations
where we might be easily tempted to disobey God.

A Family Prayer

*Heavenly Father, when we turn our thoughts away
from You and Your Word, we suffer. But when we
obey Your commandments, when we place our faith
in You, we are secure. Let us live according to
Your commandments. Direct our paths far from
the temptations and distractions of this world.
And, let us discover Your will and follow it,
Dear Lord, this day and always.
Amen*

What We Can Do as a Family

SIGN ON!

IF YOU AGREE TO THE ABOVE PLANS FOR OUR FAMILY, PLEASE SIGN YOUR NAME.

FORMING THE HABIT OF . . .

Prayer

*And everything—whatever you ask in prayer,
believing—you will receive.*

Matthew 21:22 HOLMAN CSB

D oes prayer play an important role in the life of your family? Is prayer an integral part of your daily routine or is it a hit-or-miss activity? Do you "pray without ceasing," or is your prayer life an afterthought? If you genuinely wish to receive that abundance that is available through Christ, you must pray constantly, and you must never underestimate the power of prayer.

As you contemplate the quality of your family's prayer life, here are a few things to consider: 1. God hears our prayers and answers them (Jeremiah 29:11-12). 2. God promises that the prayers of righteous people can accomplish great things (James 5:16). 3. God invites us to be still and to feel His presence (Psalm 46:10).

So pray. Pray as a family and pray individually. Start praying in the early morning and keep praying until you fall off to sleep at night. Pray about matters great and small; and be watchful for the answers that God most assuredly sends your way.

> When you ask God to do something, don't ask timidly; put your whole heart into it.
>
> Marie T. Freeman

Daily prayer and meditation is a matter of will and habit. When you organize you day to include quiet moments with God, you'll soon discover that no time is more precious than the silent moments you spend with Him.

The quality of your spiritual life will be in direct proportion to the quality of your prayer life. So do yourself and your loved ones a favor: instead of turning things over in your mind, turn them over to God in prayer. Instead of worrying about your next decision, ask God to lead the way. Don't limit your prayers to meals or to bedtime. Pray constantly because God is listening—and He wants to hear from you. And without question, you need to hear from Him.

When there is a matter that requires definite prayer, pray until you believe God and until you can thank Him for His answer.

Hannah Whitall Smith

I live in the spirit of prayer; I pray as I walk, when I lie down, and when I rise. And, the answers are always coming.

George Mueller

As we join together in prayer, we draw on God's enabling might in a way that multiplies our own efforts many times over.

Shirley Dobson

The center of power is not to be found in summit meetings or in peace conferences. It is not in Peking or Washington or the United Nations, but rather where a child of God prays in the power of the Spirit for God's will to be done in her life, in her home, and in the world around her.

Ruth Bell Graham

Yet He often withdrew to deserted places and prayed.

Luke 5:16 HOLMAN CSB

Let the words of my mouth and the meditation of my heart be acceptable in Your sight, O Lord, my strength and my Redeemer.

Psalm 19:14 NKJV

The intense prayer of the righteous is very powerful.

James 5:16 HOLMAN CSB

Rejoice always! Pray constantly. Give thanks in everything, for this is God's will for you in Christ Jesus.

1 Thessalonians 5:16-18 HCSB

Don't worry about anything, but in everything, through prayer and petition with thanksgiving, let your requests be made known to God.

Philippians 4:6 HOLMAN CSB

For More Thoughts About Prayer, Please Turn to Page 146

FAMILY VALUES

	CHECK ONE:
	YES NO

We understand that prayer strengthens our
relationship with God.

_____   _____

We trust that God will care for us, even when it
seems that our prayers have gone unanswered.

_____   _____

We believe that our prayers have the power to
change our circumstances, our perspective,
and our futures.

_____   _____

A Family Prayer

*Lord, we pray because You desire it and because
we need it. Prayer not only changes things, it also
changes us. Help us, Lord, never to face the demands
of the day without first spending time with You,
and help us make prayer a part of everything
that we do and everything that we are.*
Amen

What We Can Do as a Family

_____

_____

_____

_____

_____

_____

_____

_____

_____

_____

_____

_____

_____

_____

_____

_____

_____

_____

_____

_____

_____

SIGN ON!

IF YOU AGREE TO THE ABOVE PLANS FOR OUR FAMILY, PLEASE SIGN YOUR NAME.

FORMING THE HABIT OF . . .

Bible Study

*All Scripture is inspired by God and is profitable
for teaching, for rebuking, for correcting,
for training in righteousness, so that the man
of God may be complete, equipped for
every good work.*

2 Timothy 3:16-17 Holman CSB

I s Bible study a high priority for you and your family? The answer to this simple question will determine, to a surprising extent, the quality of your lives and the direction of your faith.

As a family, you must decide whether God's Word will be a bright spotlight that guides your path every day or a tiny nightlight that occasionally flickers in the dark. The decision to study the Bible—or not—is yours individually and collectively. But make no mistake: how your family chooses to choose the Bible will have a profound impact on every member of the household.

George Mueller observed, "The vigor of our spiritual lives will be in exact proportion to the place held by the Bible in our lives and in our thoughts." Think of it like this: the more you use your Bible, the more God uses you.

> Nobody ever outgrows Scripture; the book widens and deepens with our years.
>
> C. H. Spurgeon

Perhaps your bookshelf is filled with Bibles that are read infrequently. If so, remember the old saying, "A Bible in the hand is worth two in the bookcase." Or perhaps yours in one of those families that is simply "too busy" to find time for a daily dose of prayer and Bible study. If so, remember the old adage, "It's hard to stumble when you're on your knees."

God's Word can be a roadmap to a place of righteousness and abundance. Make it your family's roadmap. God's wisdom can be a light to guide your steps. Claim it as your family's light today, tomorrow, and every day of your life—and then walk confidently in the footsteps of God's only begotten Son.

I study the Bible as I gather apples. First, I shake the whole tree that the ripest might fall. Then I shake each limb; I shake each branch and every twig. Then, I look under every leaf.

Martin Luther

Study the Bible and observe how the persons behaved and how God dealt with them. There is explicit teaching on every condition of life.

Corrie ten Boom

Reading news without reading the Bible will inevitably lead to an unbalanced life, an anxious spirit, a worried and depressed soul.

Bill Bright

Knowing God involves an intimate, personal relationship that is developed over time through prayer and getting answers to prayer, through Bible study and applying its teaching to our lives, through obedience and experiencing the power of God, through moment-by-moment submission to Him that results in a moment-by-moment filling of the Holy Spirit.

Anne Graham Lotz

For I am not ashamed of the gospel, because it is God's power for salvation to everyone who believes.

Romans 1:16 HOLMAN CSB

Man shall not live by bread alone, but by every word that proceeds from the mouth of God.

Matthew 4:4 NKJV

Your word is a lamp for my feet and a light on my path.

Psalm 119:105 Holman CSB

Heaven and earth will pass away, but My words will never pass away.

Matthew 24:35 HOLMAN CSB

For the word of God is living and effective and sharper than any two-edged sword, penetrating as far as to divide soul, spirit, joints, and marrow; it is a judge of the ideas and thoughts of the heart.

Hebrews 4:12 HOLMAN CSB

FAMILY VALUES

	CHECK ONE:	
	YES	NO

We believe that it is important to read
the Bible every day.

_____   _____

We believe the Bible is God's instruction book
to all of mankind and for our family.

_____   _____

We consider regular Bible study to be an
important source of wisdom.

_____   _____

We have a systematic plan for studying
of God's Word.

_____   _____

A Family Prayer

*As we journey through this life, Lord, help us always
to consult the true road map: Your Holy Word.
We know that when we turn our hearts and
our thoughts to You, Father, You will lead us along
the path that is right for us. Today, dear Lord,
let us know Your will and study Your Word so that
we might understand Your plan for our lives.
Amen*

What We Can Do as a Family

_____

_____

_____

_____

_____

_____

_____

_____

_____

_____

_____

_____

_____

_____

_____

_____

_____

_____

SIGN ON!

IF YOU AGREE TO THE ABOVE PLANS FOR OUR FAMILY, PLEASE SIGN YOUR NAME.

FORMING THE HABIT OF . . .

Stewardship

*Based on the gift they have received,
everyone should use it to serve others,
as good managers of the varied grace of God.*

1 Peter 4:10 Holman CSB

Christian stewardship may be defined as "the proper management of one's resources for the glory of God." And for thoughtful believers, stewardship isn't a hit or miss proposition, it's a way of thinking and a way of living.

As Christians, we are challenged to be faithful stewards of the resources and talents that God has given us. But we live in a world that encourages us to do otherwise. Ours is a society that is filled to the brim with countless opportunities to squander our time, our talents, our energy, and our money. But we must beware: God warns us not to waste the blessings that He has bestowed upon us, and we must heed that warning.

Every member of your family possesses special gifts, unique talents and opportunities that can be used or not. You should value the talents that God has given each of you, you should nourish those talents, and you should share them with the world.

John Wesley advised, "Employ whatever God has entrusted you with, in doing good, all possible good, in every possible kind and degree." And Francis Bacon noted, "Natural abilities are like natural plants; they need pruning by study." Both observations are still valid. For dedicated Christian families like yours, talents should never be wasted and stewardship should never be taken lightly. After all, God has given you countless blessings. That's why you must manage your family's resources as if they were vitally important to God, which, by the way, they are.

> You can sing your heart out but never give back to God, and you'll miss the fullness of worship.
>
> Dave Ramsey

Christians have become victims of one of the most devious plots Satan ever created—the concept that money belongs to us and not to God.

Larry Burkett

If our charities do not at all pinch or hamper us, I should say they are too small. There ought to be things we should like to do and cannot do because our charitable expenditure excludes them.

C. S. Lewis

God will withdraw resources from the poor stewards, as related in Matthew 25, and give it to the good stewards.

Bill Bright

A steward is one who manages another's resources. Each of us is a manager, not an owner. God is the owner, and we are to manage according to His plan.

Larry Burkett

Let a man so consider us, as servants of Christ and stewards of the mysteries of God. Moreover it is required in stewards that one be found faithful.

1 Corinthians 4:1-2 NKJV

Well done, good and faithful servant; you were faithful over a few things, I will make you ruler over many things. Enter into the joy of your lord.

Matthew 25:21 NKJV

Anyone finding his life will lose it, and anyone losing his life because of Me will find it.

Matthew 10:39 HOLMAN CSB

There is therefore now no condemnation to those who are in Christ Jesus, who do not walk according to the flesh, but according to the Spirit.

Romans 8:1 NKJV

FAMILY VALUES

We understand the importance of being good
stewards of our time, our talents,
and our resources.

We trust that all our resources come from God,
and we know that He deserves the first fruits
of our labors.

We trust that when we are good stewards of
our resources, God will bless our endeavors
and our family.

CHECK ONE:	
YES	NO
_____	_____
_____	_____
_____	_____

A Family Prayer

*Dear Lord, make us faithful stewards of our
possessions. We trust, Father, that You will provide
for us now and throughout eternity. And We will obey
Your commandment that we give sacrificially to
the needs of Your Church. Thank You, Lord,
for Your gifts. Use our offerings as a blessing to others
so that Your will might be done today and forever.*
Amen

What We Can Do as a Family

_____

_____

_____

_____

_____

_____

_____

_____

_____

_____

_____

_____

_____

_____

_____

_____

_____

_____

_____

_____

SIGN ON!

_____

IF YOU AGREE TO THE ABOVE PLANS FOR OUR FAMILY, PLEASE SIGN YOUR NAME.

FORMING THE HABIT OF . . .

Forgiveness

All bitterness, anger and wrath, insult and slander must be removed from you, along with all wickedness. And be kind and compassionate to one another, forgiving one another, just as God also forgave you in Christ.

Ephesians 4:31-32 HOLMAN CSB

Here's a question for every member of the family: Do you value the role that forgiveness can play in your life? Hopefully so. But even if you're a dedicated believer, you may have a difficult time forgiving those who have hurt you. If you're one of those folks who, despite your best intentions, has a difficult time forgiving and forgetting, you are not alone.

> Bitterness is the trap that snares the hunter.
>
> Max Lucado

Life would be much simpler if we humans could forgive people "once and for all" and be done with it. But forgiveness is seldom that easy. For most of us, the decision to forgive is straightforward, but the process of forgiving is more difficult. Forgiveness is a journey that requires effort, time, perseverance, and prayer.

Sometimes, it's not "the other person" whom we need to forgive; it's ourselves. If you've made mistakes (and who among us hasn't?), perhaps you're continuing to bear a grudge against the person you see every time you look in the mirror. If so, here's a three-step process for resolving those feelings:

1. Be sure you've stopped doing whatever it is that you need to be forgiven for (got that?). 2. Seek forgiveness from God and from anybody you may have hurt. 3. Ask God to cleanse your heart of all bitterness and regret . . . and keep asking Him until you're no longer embittered.

If there exists even one person, alive or dead, whom you have not forgiven (and that includes yourself), follow God's commandment by forgiving that person today. The best time to forgive is now . . . always now.

Forgiveness is actually the best revenge because it not only sets us free from the person we forgive, but it frees us to move into all that God has in store for us.

Stormie Omartian

We are products of our past, but we don't have to be prisoners of it. God specializes in giving people a fresh start.

Rick Warren

Miracles broke the physical laws of the universe; forgiveness broke the moral rules.

Philip Yancey

Forgiveness is contagious. First you forgive them, and pretty soon, they'll forgive you, too.

Marie T. Freeman

See to it that no one repays evil for evil to anyone, but always pursue what is good for one another and for all.

1 Thessalonians 5:15 HOLMAN CSB

A person's insight gives him patience, and his virtue is to overlook an offense.

Proverbs 19:11 HOLMAN CSB

And forgive us our sins, for we ourselves also forgive everyone in debt to us.

Luke 11:4 HOLMAN CSB

Be merciful, just as your Father also is merciful.

Luke 6:36 HOLMAN CSB

For More Thoughts About Forgiveness, Please Turn to Page 148

FAMILY VALUES

	CHECK ONE:	
	YES	NO

We acknowledge the important role that
forgiveness plays in our lives.

_____ _____

We will strive to forgive those who have hurt us,
even when doing so is difficult.

_____ _____

We understand that forgiveness is a marathon
(not a sprint), and we will prayerfully ask God
to help us move beyond the emotions of
bitterness and regret.

_____ _____

We will ask God to forgive our own shortcomings,
and we will forgive ourselves for the mistakes
that we have made.

_____ _____

A Family Prayer

*Heavenly Father, forgiveness is Your commandment,
and we know that we should forgive others just as
You have forgiven us. But, genuine forgiveness is
difficult. Help us to forgive those who have injured us,
and deliver us from the traps of anger and bitterness.
Forgiveness is Your way, Lord; let it be ours.
Amen*

What We Can Do as a Family

_____
_____
_____
_____
_____
_____
_____
_____
_____
_____
_____
_____
_____
_____
_____
_____
_____
_____
_____

SIGN ON!

_____

IF YOU AGREE TO THE ABOVE PLANS FOR OUR FAMILY, PLEASE SIGN YOUR NAME.

DAY 6

FORMING THE HABIT OF . . .

Service

Worship the Lord your God and . . .
serve Him only.

Matthew 4:10 HOLMAN CSB

I f you and your family members genuinely seek to discover God's unfolding priorities for your lives, you must ask yourselves this question: "How does God want us to serve others?" And you may be certain of this: service to others is an integral part of God's plan for your lives.

Christ was the ultimate servant, the Savior who gave His life for mankind. As His followers, we, too, must become humble servants. As Christians, we are clearly (and repeatedly) instructed to assist those in need. But, as weak human beings, we sometimes fall short as we seek to puff ourselves up and glorify our own accomplishments. Jesus commands otherwise.

He teaches us that the most esteemed men and women are not the self-congratulatory leaders of society but are instead the humblest of servants.

Is your family willing to roll up its sleeves and become humble servants for Christ? Are you willing to do your part to make the world a better place? Are you

> If you aren't serving, you're just existing, because life is meant for ministry.
>
> Rick Warren

willing to serve God now and trust Him to bless you later? The answer to these questions will determine the direction of your lives and the quality of your service.

As members of God's family, we must serve our neighbors quietly and without fanfare. We must find needs and meet them. We must lend helping hands and share kind words with humility in our hearts and praise on our lips. And we must remember that every time we help someone in need, we are serving our Savior . . . which, by the way, is precisely what we must do.

Through our service to others, God wants to influence our world for Him.

Vonette Bright

God will open up places of service for you as He sees you are ready. Meanwhile, study the Bible and give yourself a chance to grow.

Warren Wiersbe

Christianity, in its purest form, is nothing more than seeing Jesus. Christian service, in its purest form, is nothing more than imitating Him who we see. To see His Majesty and to imitate Him: that is the sum of Christianity.

Max Lucado

So many times we say that we can't serve God because we aren't whatever is needed. We're not talented enough or smart enough or whatever. But if you are in covenant with Jesus Christ, He is responsible for covering your weaknesses, for being your strength. He will give you His abilities for your disabilities!

Kay Arthur

A person should consider us in this way: as servants of Christ and managers of God's mysteries. In this regard, it is expected of managers that each one be found faithful.

1 Corinthians 4:1-2 HOLMAN CSB

If they serve Him obediently, they will end their days in prosperity and their years in happiness.

Job 36:11 HOLMAN CSB

We must do the works of Him who sent Me while it is day. Night is coming when no one can work.

John 9:4 HOLMAN CSB

Serve the Lord with gladness.

Psalm 100:2 HOLMAN CSB

For More Thoughts About Service, Please Turn to Page 150

FAMILY VALUES

	CHECK ONE:	
	YES	NO

Christ was a humble servant, and we value the importance of following His example . . .

_____ _____

We understand that greatness in God's kingdom relates to service, not status . . .

_____ _____

We will be proactive in our search to find ways to help others . . .

_____ _____

A Family Prayer

Dear Lord, in weak moments, we may try to build ourselves up by placing ourselves ahead of others. But You want us to be humble servants to those who need our encouragement, our help, and our love. Today, we will do our best to follow in the footsteps of Your Son Jesus by serving others humbly, faithfully, and lovingly.
Amen

What We Can Do as a Family

_____

_____

_____

_____

_____

_____

_____

_____

_____

_____

_____

_____

_____

_____

_____

_____

_____

_____

_____

_____

SIGN ON!

IF YOU AGREE TO THE ABOVE PLANS FOR OUR FAMILY, PLEASE SIGN YOUR NAME.

DAY 7

FORMING THE HABIT OF . . .

Praise

and

thanksgiving

It is good to give thanks to the Lord,
And to sing praises to Your name,
O Most High.

Psalm 92:1 NKJV

God has blessed your family beyond measure, and you owe Him everything, including your constant praise. That's why thanksgiving should become a habit, a regular part of your family's daily routine. Dietrich Bonhoeffer observed, "It is only with gratitude that life becomes rich." These words most certainly apply to you and yours.

As a followers of Christ, you have been blessed beyond measure. God sent His only Son to die for you. And, God has given you the priceless gifts of eternal love and eternal life. You, in turn, should approach your Heavenly Father with reverence and gratitude.

Is your family sufficiently grateful for God's blessings? Do you thank Him many times each day for the opportunities that He has given you? And, do you demonstrate your gratitude by being faithful stewards of your time, your talents, and your resources? Hopefully, the answer to these questions is yes.

> The joy of the Holy Spirit is experienced by giving thanks in all situations.
>
> Bill Bright

Billy Graham had this advice for believers of all ages: "Think of the blessings we so easily take for granted: Life itself; preservation from danger; every bit of health we enjoy; every hour of liberty; the ability to see, to hear, to speak, to think, and to imagine all this comes from the hand of God." And he was right. You most certainly should be thankful to God. After all, when you stop to think about it, the Creator has given you more blessings than you can count. So the question of the day is this: will you thank your Heavenly Father . . . or will you spend your time and energy doing other things?

God is always listening—are you willing to say thanks? It's up to you and your family . . . and the next move is yours.

Praise and thank God for who He is and for what He has done for you.

Billy Graham

It is always possible to be thankful for what is given rather than to complain about what is not given. One or the other becomes a habit of life.

Elisabeth Elliot

The act of thanksgiving is a demonstration of the fact that you are going to trust and believe God.

Kay Arthur

God is worthy of our praise and is pleased when we come before Him with thanksgiving.

Shirley Dobson

Thanks be to God for His indescribable gift.

2 Corinthians 9:15 HOLMAN CSB

And let the peace of the Messiah, to which you were also called in one body, control your hearts. Be thankful.

Colossians 3:15 HOLMAN CSB

Therefore as you have received Christ Jesus the Lord, walk in Him, rooted and built up in Him and established in the faith, just as you were taught, and overflowing with thankfulness.

Colossians 2:6-7 HOLMAN CSB

Enter into His gates with thanksgiving, and into His courts with praise. Be thankful to Him, and bless His name. For the Lord is good; His mercy is everlasting, and His truth endures to all generations.

Psalm 100:4-5 NKJV

For More Thoughts About Praise and Thanksgiving,
Please Turn to Page 152

FAMILY VALUES

We will not take our blessings for granted.

We will remain humble as we praise God and thank Him for His gifts.

We will not only thank God for His gifts, we will use those gifts as one way of honoring Him.

We expect God's continued blessings on our family.

CHECK ONE:	
YES	NO
___	___
___	___
___	___
___	___

A Family Prayer

Dear Lord, sometimes, amid the demands of the day, we lose perspective, and we fail to give thanks for Your blessings and for Your love. Today, help us count those blessings, and let us give thanks to You, Father, for Your love, for Your grace, for Your blessings, and for Your Son.
Amen

What We Can Do as a Family

SIGN ON!

IF YOU AGREE TO THE ABOVE PLANS FOR OUR FAMILY, PLEASE SIGN YOUR NAME.

DAY 8

FORMING THE HABIT OF . . .

Sharing

God's Love

For God loved the world in this way:
He gave His only Son, so that everyone
who believes in Him will not perish
but have eternal life.

John 3:16 HOLMAN CSB

The words of 1 John 4:8 teach us that "He who does not love does not know God, for God is love" (NKJV). And because we can be assured that God is love, we can also be assured that God's heart is a loving heart.

God loves you and your family. He loves you more than you can imagine; His affection is deeper than you can fathom. God made you in His own image and gave you salvation through the person of His Son Jesus Christ. And as a result, you and your loved ones have an important decision to make. You must decide what to do about God's love: you can return it . . . or not.

> As God's children, we are the recipients of lavish love— a love that motivates us to keep trusting even when we have no idea what God is doing.
>
> Beth Moore

When you accept the love that flows from the heart of God, you are transformed. When you embrace God's love, you feel differently about yourselves, your family, your neighbors, your community, your church, and your world. When you open your heart to God's love, you will feel compelled to share God's message—and His compassion—with others.

Corrie ten Boom observed, "We must mirror God's love in the midst of a world full of hatred. We are the mirrors of God's love, so we may show Jesus by our lives." And her words still apply.

God's heart is overflowing with love for you and yours. Accept that love. Return that love. Respect that love. And share that love. Today.

God's love is measureless. It is more: it is boundless. It has no bounds because it is not a thing but a facet of the essential nature of God. His love is something he is, and because he is infinite, that love can enfold the whole created world in itself and have room for ten thousand times ten thousand worlds beside.

A. W. Tozer

Every tiny bit of my life that has value I owe to the redemption of Jesus Christ. Am I doing anything to enable Him to bring His redemption into evident reality in the lives of others?

Oswald Chambers

If you are going to live in peace, you need to embrace in faith the reality that "the LORD is in His holy temple." Embrace it and be silent before Him. You don't need to argue. You don't need to defend God. Simply explain Him as the Word of God explains Him. Then it is the skeptic's responsibility to accept or reject the Word of God. The responsibility is his, not yours. It's between him and God. It's a matter of faith.

Kay Arthur

There are many timid souls whom we jostle morning and evening as we pass them by; but if only the kind word were spoken they might become fully persuaded.

Fanny Crosby

You are the light of the world. A city that is set on a hill cannot be hidden. Nor do they light a lamp and put it under a basket, but on a lampstand, and it gives light to all who are in the house. Let your light so shine before men, that they may see your good works and glorify your Father in heaven.

Matthew 5:14–16 NKJV

Sanctify the Lord God in your hearts: and be ready always to give an answer to every man that asketh you a reason of the hope that is in you....

1 Peter 3:15 KJV

Whoever is wise will observe these things, and they will understand the lovingkindness of the Lord.

Psalm 107:43 NKJV

For the Lord is good, and His love is eternal; His faithfulness endures through all generations.

Psalm 100:5 Holman CSB

For More Thoughts About Love, Please Turn to Page 154

FAMILY VALUES

	CHECK ONE:	
	YES	NO

We know that God loves us.

We understand the importance of a loving
relationship with God by spending time with Him.

We understand the importance of sharing God's
love with our family and friends.

A Family Prayer

*Dear Heavenly Father, You have blessed us with
a love that is infinite and eternal. We will be
Your loving servants, Father, today and throughout
eternity. And, we will show our love for You
by sharing Your message and Your love with
a world that desperately needs the healing touch
of the Master's hand.*
Amen

What We Can Do as a Family

_____

_____

_____

_____

_____

_____

_____

_____

_____

_____

_____

_____

_____

_____

_____

_____

_____

_____

SIGN ON!

IF YOU AGREE TO THE ABOVE PLANS FOR OUR FAMILY, PLEASE SIGN YOUR NAME.

FORMING THE HABIT OF . . .

Worship

But an hour is coming, and is now here,
when the true worshipers will worship
the Father in spirit and truth. Yes, the Father
wants such people to worship Him.
God is Spirit, and those who worship Him
must worship in spirit and truth.

John 4:23-24 HOLMAN CSB

Why do you and your family members attend church? Is it because of your sincere desire to worship and to praise God? Hopefully so. Yet far too many Christians attend worship services because they believe they are "supposed to go to church" or because they feel "pressured" to attend. Still others go to church for "social" reasons. But make no mistake: the best reason to attend church is out of a sincere desire to please God, to praise God, to experience God, and to discern God's will for your lives.

Some people may tell you that they don't engage in worship. Don't believe them. All of mankind is engaged in worship. The question is not whether we worship, but what we worship. Wise folks choose to worship God. When they do, they are blessed with a plentiful harvest of joy, peace, and abundance. Other people choose to distance themselves from God by foolishly worshiping things

> The fact that we were created to enjoy God and to worship him forever is etched upon our souls.
>
> Jim Cymbala

that are intended to bring personal gratification but not spiritual gratification. Such choices often have tragic consequences.

If we place our love for material possessions or social status above our love for God—or if we yield to the countless temptations of this world—we find ourselves engaged in a struggle between good and evil, a clash between God and Satan. Our responses to these struggles have implications that echo throughout our families and throughout our communities.

How can we ensure that we cast our lot with God? We do so, in part, by the practice of regular, purposeful worship in the company of fellow believers. When we worship God faithfully and fervently, we are blessed. When we fail to worship God, for whatever reason, we forfeit the spiritual gifts that might otherwise be ours.

We must worship our heavenly Father, not just with our words, but also with deeds. We must honor Him, praise Him, and obey Him. As we seek to find purpose and meaning for our lives, we must first seek His purpose and His will. For believers, God comes first. Always first.

It's the definition of worship: A hungry heart finding the Father's feast. A searching soul finding the Father's face. A wandering pilgrim spotting the Father's house. Finding God. Finding God seeking us. This is worship. This is a worshiper.

Max Lucado

Some people are so busy observing ritual that they never get to know God personally. Ritual must bring me to close personal contact with God, or it's useless.

Grady Nutt

So that at the name of Jesus every knee should bow—of those who are in heaven and on earth and under the earth—and every tongue should confess that Jesus Christ is Lord, to the glory of God the Father.

Philippians 2:10-11 HOLMAN CSB

Worship the Lord your God and . . . serve Him only.

Matthew 4:10 HOLMAN CSB

If anyone is thirsty, he should come to Me and drink!

John 7:37 HOLMAN CSB

And every day they devoted themselves to meeting together in the temple complex, and broke bread from house to house. They ate their food with gladness and simplicity of heart, praising God and having favor with all the people. And every day the Lord added those being saved to them.

Acts 2:46-47 HOLMAN CSB

For More Thoughts About Worship, Please Turn to Page 156

FAMILY VALUES

	CHECK ONE:	
	YES	NO

We will consider each day an opportunity to praise God and to worship Him.

____ ____

We will be actively involved in our church.

____ ____

We will consider praise and worship to be a regular part of our day.

____ ____

We will worship God in spirit and truth.

____ ____

A Family Prayer

*When we worship You, Lord, You direct our paths
and You cleanse our hearts. Let today and every day
be a time of worship and praise. Let us worship You in
everything that we think and do. Thank You, Lord,
for the priceless gift of Your Son Jesus. Let us be
worthy of that gift, and let us give You
the praise and the glory forever.*
Amen

What We Can Do as a Family

SIGN ON!

IF YOU AGREE TO THE ABOVE PLANS FOR OUR FAMILY, PLEASE SIGN YOUR NAME.

PART 2

Your Family's PHYSICAL HEALTH

Life is a gift—health must be earned.
We earn good health by cultivating
healthy habits.

FORMING THE HABIT OF . . .

A Healthy Diet

Therefore, whether you eat or drink,
or whatever you do,
do everything for God's glory.

1 Corinthians 10:31 HOLMAN CSB

E ating unhealthy foods is habit-forming. And if you or your family members have acquired the unfortunate habit of eating unhealthy foods, then God wants you to start making changes today.

Take a few minutes to think about your family's eating habits. Do you gobble down snack foods while watching television? If so, stop. Do you drink high calorie soft drinks or feast on unhealthy snacks like potato chips or candy? If so, you're doing yourself a disservice. Do you delight in high fat, high calorie foods that taste good for a few seconds but accumulate on your waistlines for years?

> We should take twice as long to eat half as much.
>
> Anonymous

Do you load up your plate until food falls off the edge? And then do you feel obligated to eat every last bite? If so, it's time to think long and hard about the serious consequences of indulging in unhealthy habits.

Poor eating habits are easy to make and hard to break, but break them you must. Otherwise, you'll be disobeying God's commandments while causing yourselves great harm.

Maintaining a healthy lifestyle is a journey, not a destination, and that journey requires discipline. But rest assured that if you and your loved ones are willing to make the step-by-step journey toward a healthier diet, God is taking careful note of your progress . . . and He's quietly urging you to take the next step.

People are funny. When they are young, they will spend their health to get wealth. Later, they will gladly pay all they have trying to get their health back.

John Maxwell

A Christian should no more defile his body than a Jew would defile the temple.

Warren Wiersbe

Eat to live, and not live to eat.

Poor Richard's Almanac

Always rise from the table with an appetite, and you will never sit down without one.

William Penn

But I discipline my body and bring it into subjection, lest, when I have preached to others, I myself should become disqualified.

1 Corinthians 9:27 NKJV

The Lord is the strength of my life.

Psalm 27:1 KJV

Beloved, I pray that you may prosper in all things and be in health, just as your soul prospers.

3 John 1:2 NKJV

Acquire wisdom—how much better it is than gold! And acquire understanding—it is preferable to silver.

Proverbs 16:16 HCSB

FAMILY VALUES

	CHECK ONE:	
	YES	NO

We understand that our bodies are priceless gifts from God.

    ———   ———

We know that we should treat our bodies with the utmost care.

    ———   ———

We understand the importance of eating healthy foods.

    ———   ———

We understand the need to be moderate, not gluttonous.

    ———   ———

A Family Prayer

Dear Lord, You teach us that we should treat our bodies as temples. Keep us mindful that the foods we eat are important to our health, and that if we are to treat our bodies with respect, we should eat healthy foods in sensible amounts.

Amen

What We Can Do as a Family

SIGN ON!

IF YOU AGREE TO THE ABOVE PLANS FOR OUR FAMILY, PLEASE SIGN YOUR NAME.

FORMING THE HABIT OF . . .

Sensible

Exercise

Therefore, brothers, by the mercies of God,
I urge you to present your bodies as
a living sacrifice, holy and pleasing to God;
this is your spiritual worship.

Romans 12:1 HOLMAN CSB

A re you shaping up or spreading out? Do you exercise regularly, or do you spend most of your time on the couch with a Twinkie in one hand and a clicker in the other? Are you and your loved ones choosing to treat your bodies like temples—or not? How you answer these questions will help determine how long you live and how well you live.

Physical fitness is a choice, a choice that requires discipline—it's as simple as that. But here's the catch: understanding the need for discipline is easy, but leading a disciplined life can be hard. Why? Because it's usually more fun to eat a second piece of cake than it is to jog a second lap around the track. Nonetheless, as we survey the second helpings that all too often find their way on to our plates, we should consider this: as Christians, we are instructed to lead disciplined lives, and when we behave in undisciplined ways, we are living outside God's will.

> Making up a string of excuses is usually harder than doing the work.
>
> Marie T. Freeman

We live in a world in which leisure is glorified and consumption is commercialized. But God has other plans. He did not create us for lives of gluttony or laziness; He created us for far greater things.

God has a plan for every aspect of your life, and His plan includes provisions for your physical health—and that means regular, sensible exercise. How much exercise is right for you? That's a decision that you should make in consultation with your physician. But make no mistake: if you sincerely desire to be a thoughtful caretaker of the body that God has given you, exercise is important.

Once you begin a regular exercise program, you'll discover that the benefits to you are not only physical but also psychological. Regular exercise allows you to build your muscles while you're clearing your head and lifting your spirits.

So, if you or your loved ones have been taking your bodies for granted, today is a wonderful day to change. You can start slowly, perhaps with a brisk walk around the block. As your stamina begins to build, so too will your sense of satisfaction. And, you'll be comforted by the knowledge that you've done your part to protect and preserve the precious body that God has entrusted to your care.

Most people I know either love exercise and do it excessively, or they hate it and avoid it completely; yet consistent exercise is one of the keys to good health.

John Maxwell

God wants you to give Him your body. Some people do foolish things with their bodies. God wants your body as a holy sacrifice.

Warren Wiersbe

Don't you know that you are God's sanctuary and that the Spirit of God lives in you?

1 Corinthians 3:16 HOLMAN CSB

For You formed my inward parts; You covered me in my mother's womb. I will praise You, for I am fearfully and wonderfully made; Marvelous are Your works.

Psalm 139:13-14 NKJV

The one who walks with the wise will become wise, but a companion of fools will suffer harm.

Proverbs 13:20 HCSB

Do you not know that your body is a sanctuary of the Holy Spirit who is in you, whom you have from God? You are not your own, for you were bought at a price; therefore glorify God in your body.

1 Corinthians 6:19-20 HOLMAN CSB

FAMILY VALUES

	CHECK ONE:	
	YES	NO

We understand the importance of
sensible exercise.

_____ _____

We strive to make exercise enjoyable.

_____ _____

We understand that every member of our family
should be engaged in a program of regular
physical exercise.

_____ _____

A Family Prayer

*Dear Lord, our bodies are, indeed, priceless gifts
from you. Help us treat our bodies with care.
Keep us mindful that all our gifts come from you,
and let us be good stewards of those gifts
today and everyday.
Amen*

What We Can Do as a Family

SIGN ON!

IF YOU AGREE TO THE ABOVE PLANS FOR OUR FAMILY, PLEASE SIGN YOUR NAME.

DAY 12

FORMING THE HABIT OF . . .

Getting Enough Sleep

But those who wait on the Lord shall renew their strength; They shall mount up with wings like eagles, They shall run and not be weary, They shall walk and not faint.

Isaiah 40:31 NKJV

The demands of everyday living can drain us of our strength and rob us of the joy that is rightfully ours in Christ.

God intends that His children lead joyous lives filled with abundance and peace. But sometimes, abundance and peace seem very far away. It is during these darker moments that we must turn to God for renewal, and when we do, He will restore us.

Physical exhaustion is God's way of telling us to slow down. God expects us to work hard, of course, but He also intends for us to rest. When we fail to take the rest that we need, we do a disservice to ourselves and to our families.

> Life is strenuous. See that your clock does not run down.
>
> Mrs. Charles E. Cowman

We live in a world that tempts us to stay up late—very late. But too much late-night TV, combined with too little sleep, is a prescription for exhaustion—and it's a prescription that you should avoid. Otherwise, you'll find yourself running short of energy, short on patience, and short on perspective.

Are your physical or spiritual batteries running low? Is your energy on the wane? Are your emotions frayed? If so, it's time to turn your thoughts and your prayers to God. And when you're finished, it's probably time to turn off the lights and go to bed!

Prescription for a happier and healthier life: resolve to slow down your pace; learn to say no gracefully; resist the temptation to chase after more pleasure, more hobbies, and more social entanglements.

James Dobson

Satan does some of his worst work on exhausted Christians when nerves are frayed and their minds are faint.

Vance Havner

Taking care of yourself physically really helps emotionally. People who get a lot of sleep, who do the things that relieve stress, can withstand a lot of stress.

Laura Bush

All that a Christian does, even in eating and sleeping, is prayer, when it is done in simplicity, according to the order of God, without either adding to or diminishing from it by His choice.

John Wesley

But may the God of all grace, who called us to His eternal glory by Christ Jesus, after you have suffered a while, perfect, establish, strengthen, and settle you.

1 Peter 5:10 NKJV

Come to Me, all you who labor and are heavy laden, and I will give you rest. Take My yoke upon you and learn from Me, for I am gentle and lowly in heart, and you will find rest for your souls. For My yoke is easy and My burden is light.

Matthew 11:28-30 NKJV

You are being renewed in the spirit of your minds; you put on the new man, the one created according to God's likeness in righteousness and purity of the truth.

Ephesians 4:23-24 HOLMAN CSB

Rest in God alone, my soul, for my hope comes from Him.

Psalm 62:5 HOLMAN CSB

FAMILY VALUES

	CHECK ONE:	
	YES	NO

We understand the need for adequate rest.

We plan our family activities in order that every member of our family gets to bed at an hour that allows for sufficient sleep.

We understand that we all feel better and function better when we're rested.

A Family Prayer

Dear Lord, when we are tempted to burn the candle at both ends, give us the wisdom to do the sensible thing—give us the wisdom to put our heads on our pillows and rest.
Amen

What We Can Do as a Family

_____

_____

_____

_____

_____

_____

_____

_____

_____

_____

_____

_____

_____

_____

_____

_____

_____

_____

SIGN ON!

IF YOU AGREE TO THE ABOVE PLANS FOR OUR FAMILY. PLEASE SIGN YOUR NAME.

FORMING THE HABIT OF . . .

Observing a Day of Rest

Remember the Sabbath day, to keep it holy.

Exodus 20:8 NKJV

When God gave Moses the Ten Commandments, it became perfectly clear that our Heavenly Father intends for His children to make the Sabbath a holy day, a day for worship, for contemplation, for fellowship, and for rest. Yet we live in a seven-day-a-week world, a world that all too often treats Sunday as a bonus shopping day and a regular workday. But the Lord's day deserves to be respected by those who choose to follow the Son of God.

You and your family members will face powerful temptations, temptations to rush through Sunday services and get on with "business as usual." The world wants you to make Sunday a time for shopping, a time for working, a time for rushing from place to place with scarcely a moment to spare. But God wants you to make the Sabbath a special day—and that's precisely what you should want for you and your family.

> Jesus taught us by example to get out of the rat race and recharge our batteries.
>
> Barbara Johnson

How does your family observe the Lord's day? When church is over, do you treat Sunday like any other day of the week? If so, it's time to think long and hard about your family's schedule and your family's priorities.

Whenever we ignore God's commandments, we pay a price. So if you've been treating Sunday as just another day, it's time to break that habit. When Sunday rolls around, don't try to fill every spare moment. Take time to worship and to rest . . . Father's orders!

Jesus gives us the ultimate rest, the confidence we need, to escape the frustration and chaos of the world around us.

Billy Graham

It is what Jesus is, not what we are, that gives rest to the soul. If we really want to overcome Satan and have peace with God, we must "fix our eyes on Jesus." Let his death, his suffering, his glories, and his intercession be fresh on your mind.

C. H. Spurgeon

One reason so much American Christianity is a mile wide and an inch deep is that Christians are simply tired. Sometimes you need to kick back and rest for Jesus' sake.

Dennis Swanberg

Come, come, come unto Me, weary and sore distressed; come, come, come unto Me, come unto Me and rest.

Fanny Crosby

THE TEN COMMANDMENTS

Then God spoke all these words: I am the Lord your God, who brought you out of the land of Egypt, out of the place of slavery. Do not have other gods besides Me. Do not make an idol for yourself, whether in the shape of anything in the heavens above or on the earth below or in the waters under the earth. You must not bow down to them or worship them; for I, the Lord your God, am a jealous God, punishing the children for the fathers' sin, to the third and fourth [generations] of those who hate Me, but showing faithful love to a thousand [generations] of those who love Me and keep My commands. Do not misuse the name of the Lord your God, because the Lord will punish anyone who misuses His name. Remember to dedicate the Sabbath day: You are to labor six days and do all your work, but the seventh day is a Sabbath to the Lord your God. You must not do any work-you, your son or daughter, your male or female slave, your livestock, or the foreigner who is within your gates. For the Lord made the heavens and the earth, the sea, and everything in them in six days; then He rested on the seventh day. Therefore the Lord blessed the Sabbath day and declared it holy. Honor your father and your mother so that you may have a long life in the land that the Lord your God is giving you. Do not murder. Do not commit adultery. Do not steal. Do not give false testimony against your neighbor. Do not covet your neighbor's house. Do not covet your neighbor's wife, his male or female slave, his ox or donkey, or anything that belongs to your neighbor.

Exodus 20:1-17 HOLMAN CSB

FAMILY VALUES

	CHECK ONE:	
	YES	NO

We respect God's commandment that one day
a week should be His.

We believe that Sunday is a special day,
and we treat it that way.

We reserve Sunday as a time of worship,
praise, reflection, fellowship, and rest.

A Family Prayer

Dear Lord, we thank You for the Sabbath day,
a day when we can worship You and praise Your Son.
We will keep the Sabbath as a holy day,
a day when we can honor You.
Amen

What We Can Do as a Family

_____

_____

_____

_____

_____

_____

_____

_____

_____

_____

_____

_____

_____

_____

_____

_____

_____

_____

_____

_____

SIGN ON!

_____

IF YOU AGREE TO THE ABOVE PLANS FOR OUR FAMILY, PLEASE SIGN YOUR NAME.

PART 3

Your Family's EMOTIONAL HEALTH

Emotions are contagious.
As members of a loving family,
we should make certain that the emotions
we share are the healthy kind.

DAY 14

FORMING THE HABIT OF . . .

Encouraging Others

*I want their hearts to be encouraged
and joined together in love, so that they may
have all the riches of assured understanding,
and have the knowledge of
God's mystery—Christ.*

Colossians 2:2 HOLMAN CSB

The ninth chapter of John reminds us that, "I must work the works of Him who sent Me while it is day; the night is coming when no one can work" (v. 4 NKJV). And we must remember that an important part of today's work includes celebrating the victories of others. Each day provides countless opportunities to encourage others and to praise their good works. When we do, we not only spread seeds of joy and happiness, we also follow the commandments of God's Holy Word.

In his letter to the Ephesians, Paul writes, "No rotten talk should come from your mouth, but only what is good for the building up of someone in need, in order to give grace to those who hear." (4:29 HOLMAN CSB). This passage reminds us that, as Christians, we are instructed to choose our words carefully so as to build others up through wholesome, honest encouragement. How can we build others up? By celebrating their victories and their accomplishments. As the old saying goes, "When someone does something good, applaud—you'll make two people happy."

> People who inspire others are those who see invisible bridges at the end of dead-end streets.
>
> Charles Swindoll

Today, look for the good in others and celebrate the good that you find. When you do, you'll be a powerful force of encouragement in the world...and worthy servants to your God.

Overcoming discouragement is simply a matter of taking away the DIS and adding the EN.

Barbara Johnson

Make it a rule, and pray to God to help you to keep it, never to lie down at night without being able to say: "I have made at least one human being a little wiser, a little happier, or a little better this day."

Charles Kingsley

The glory of friendship is not the outstretched hand, or the kindly smile, or the joy of companionship. It is the spiritual inspiration that comes to one when he discovers that someone else believes in him and is willing to trust him with his friendship.

Corrie ten Boom

Encouraging others means helping people, looking for the best in them, and trying to bring out their positive qualities.

John Maxwell

And let us be concerned about one another in order to promote love and good works.

Hebrews 10:24 HOLMAN CSB

Carry one another's burdens; in this way you will fulfill the law of Christ.

Galatians 6:2 HOLMAN CSB

But encourage each other daily, while it is still called today, so that none of you is hardened by sin's deception.

Hebrews 3:13 HOLMAN CSB

Iron sharpens iron, and one man sharpens another.

Proverbs 27:17 HOLMAN CSB

For More Thoughts About Encouragement, Please Turn to Page 158

FAMILY VALUES

	CHECK ONE:	
	YES	NO

We believe that God wants us to encourage other people.

_____   _____

We carefully think about the words we speak so that every word might be a "gift of encouragement" to others.

_____   _____

We believe that our words reflect our hearts. We will guard our hearts so that our words will be pleasing to God.

_____   _____

A Family Prayer

Lord, make us mindful of our words. This world can be a difficult place, and many of Your children are discouraged and afraid. Make each member of our family a powerful source of encouragement to those in need, and let our words and deeds be worthy of Your Son, the One who gives us courage and strength, this day and for all eternity.
Amen

What We Can Do as a Family

SIGN ON!

IF YOU AGREE TO THE ABOVE PLANS FOR OUR FAMILY, PLEASE SIGN YOUR NAME.

FORMING THE HABIT OF . . .

Thinking Clearly

Finally brothers, whatever is true, whatever is honorable, whatever is just, whatever is pure, whatever is lovely, whatever is commendable— if there is any moral excellence and if there is any praise—dwell on these things.

Philippians 4:8 HOLMAN CSB

Thoughts are intensely powerful things. Our thoughts have the power to lift us up or drag us down; they have the power to energize us or deplete us, to inspire us to greater accomplishments or to make those accomplishments impossible.

How will you and your family members direct your thoughts today? Will you obey the words of Philippians 4:8 by dwelling upon those things that are honorable, true, and worthy of praise? Or will you allow your thoughts to be hijacked by the negativity that seems to dominate our troubled world?

Are you fearful, angry, bored, or worried? Are you so preoccupied with the concerns of this day that you fail to thank God for the promise of eternity? Are you confused, bitter, or pessimistic? If so, God wants to have a little talk with you.

> It is the thoughts and intents of the heart that shape a person's life.
>
> John Eldredge

God intends that you experience joy and abundance, but He will not force His joy upon you; you must claim it for yourself. It's up to you and your loved ones to celebrate the life that God has given you by focusing your minds upon "whatever is commendable." So form the habit of spending more time thinking about your blessings and less time fretting about your hardships. Then, take time to thank the Giver of all things good for gifts that are, in truth, far too numerous to count.

As we have by faith said no to sin, so we should by faith say yes to God and set our minds on things above, where Christ is seated in the heavenlies.

Vonette Bright

No more imperfect thoughts. No more sad memories. No more ignorance. My redeemed body will have a redeemed mind. Grant me a foretaste of that perfect mind as you mirror your thoughts in me today.

Joni Eareckson Tada

The things we think are the things that feed our souls. If we think on pure and lovely things, we shall grow pure and lovely like them; and the converse is equally true.

Hannah Whitall Smith

Your thoughts are the determining factor as to whose mold you are conformed to. Control your thoughts and you control the direction of your life.

Charles Stanley

For God has not given us a spirit of fearfulness, but one of power, love, and sound judgment.

2 Timothy 1:7 HOLMAN CSB

Set your minds on what is above, not on what is on the earth.

Colossians 3:2 HOLMAN CSB

I, the Lord, examine the mind, I test the heart to give to each according to his way, according to what his actions deserve.

Jeremiah 17:10 HOLMAN CSB

Brothers, don't be childish in your thinking, but be infants in evil and adult in your thinking.

1 Corinthians 14:20 HOLMAN CSB

For More Thoughts About Attitude, Please Turn to Page 160

FAMILY VALUES

	CHECK ONE:
	YES NO

We understand the importance of directing our thoughts in positive directions.

_____ _____

We believe that emotions are contagious, so we try to associate with people who are upbeat, optimistic, and encouraging.

_____ _____

We trust that when we dwell on positive thoughts and when we focus on God's blessings, we will feel better about ourselves and our circumstances.

_____ _____

A Family Prayer

Dear Lord, keep our thoughts focused on Your love,
Your power, Your Promises, and Your Son.
When we are worried, we will turn to You for comfort;
when we are weak, we will turn to You for strength;
when we are troubled, we will turn to You for patience
and perspective. Help us guard our thoughts,
Father, so that we may honor You
today and every day that we live.
Amen

What We Can Do as a Family

_____

_____

_____

_____

_____

_____

_____

_____

_____

_____

_____

_____

_____

_____

_____

_____

SIGN ON!

IF YOU AGREE TO THE ABOVE PLANS FOR OUR FAMILY, PLEASE SIGN YOUR NAME.

FORMING THE HABIT OF . . .

Celebrating Life

This is the day the LORD has made;
we will rejoice and be glad in it.

Psalm 118:24 NKJV

Today is a non-renewable resource—once it's gone, it's gone forever. Our responsibility, as thoughtful believers, is to use this day in the service of God's will and in the service of His people. When we do so, we enrich our own lives and the lives of those whom we love.

God has richly blessed us, and He wants you to rejoice in His gifts. That's why this day—and each day that follows— should be a time of prayer and celebration as we consider the Good News of God's free gift: salvation through Jesus Christ.

Oswald Chambers correctly observed, "Joy is the great note all throughout the Bible." E. Stanley Jones echoed that thought when he wrote "Christ and joy go together." But, even the most dedicated Christians can, on occasion, forget to celebrate each day for what it is: a priceless gift from God.

> Life is a glorious opportunity.
>
> Billy Graham

What do you expect from the day ahead? Are you expecting God to do wonderful things, or are you living beneath a cloud of apprehension and doubt? The familiar words of Psalm 118:24 remind us of a profound yet simple truth: "This is the day which the LORD hath made" (KJV). Our duty, as believers, is to rejoice in God's marvelous creation.

Today, celebrate the life that God has given you. Today, put a smile on your face, kind words on your lips, and a song in your heart. Be generous with your praise and free with your encouragement. And then, when you have celebrated life to the full, invite your friends to do likewise. After all, this is God's day, and He has given us clear instructions for its use. We are commanded to rejoice and be glad. So, with no further ado, let the celebration begin…

If you can forgive the person you were, accept the person you are, and believe in the person you will become, you are headed for joy. So celebrate your life.

Barbara Johnson

Some of us seem so anxious about avoiding hell that we forget to celebrate our journey toward heaven.

Philip Yancey

The happiest people in the world are not those who have no problems, but the people who have learned to live with those things that are less than perfect.

James Dobson

Christ is the secret, the source, the substance, the center, and the circumference of all true and lasting gladness.

Mrs. Charles E. Cowman

Rejoice in the Lord always. I will say it again: Rejoice!

Philippians 4:4 HOLMAN CSB

David and the whole house of Israel were celebrating before the Lord.

2 Samuel 6:5 HOLMAN CSB

Their sorrow was turned into rejoicing and their mourning into a holiday. They were to be days of feasting, rejoicing, and of sending gifts to one another and the poor.

Esther 9:22 HOLMAN CSB

At the dedication of the wall of Jerusalem, they sent for the Levites wherever they lived and brought them to Jerusalem to celebrate the joyous dedication with thanksgiving and singing accompanied by cymbals, harps, and lyres.

Nehemiah 12:27 HOLMAN CSB

For More Thoughts About Celebrating Life, Please Turn to Page 162

FAMILY VALUES

	CHECK ONE:	
	YES	NO
We understand that every day can and should be a cause for celebration.	_____	_____
We will strive to worry less and trust God more.	_____	_____
We will share our enthusiasm with our family members, with our friends, and with the world.	_____	_____

A Family Prayer

Dear Lord, help us remember that every day is cause for celebration. Today we will try our best to keep joy in our hearts. We will celebrate the life You have given us here on earth and the eternal life that will be ours in heaven.

Amen

What We Can Do as a Family

_____

_____

_____

_____

_____

_____

_____

_____

_____

_____

_____

_____

_____

_____

_____

_____

_____

_____

SIGN ON!

IF YOU AGREE TO THE ABOVE PLANS FOR OUR FAMILY. PLEASE SIGN YOUR NAME.

FORMING THE HABIT OF . . .

Patience

Rejoice in hope; be patient in affliction;
be persistent in prayer.

Romans 12:12 Holman CSB

The dictionary defines the word patience as "the ability to be calm, tolerant, and understanding." If that describes you and your family members, you can skip today's reading and move on to the next chapter. But, if you and your loved ones could use a little extra dose of patience from time to time, read on.

For most of us, patience is a hard thing to master. Why? Because we have lots of things we want, and we know precisely when we want them: NOW (if not sooner). But our Father in heaven has other ideas; the Bible teaches that we must learn to wait patiently for the things that God has in store for us, even when waiting is difficult.

> Waiting means going about our assigned tasks, confident that God will provide the meaning and the conclusions.
>
> Eugene Peterson

We live in an imperfect world inhabited by imperfect people. Sometimes, we inherit troubles from others, and sometimes we create troubles for ourselves. On other occasions, we see other people "moving ahead" in the world, and we want to move ahead with them. So we become impatient with ourselves, with our circumstances, and even with our Creator.

Psalm 37:7 commands us to "rest in the Lord, and wait patiently for Him" (NKJV). But, for most of us, waiting patiently for Him is hard. We seek immediate solutions to our problems, and we want those solutions today, not tomorrow. Still, God instructs us to wait patiently for His plans to unfold, and that's exactly what we should do.

Sometimes, patience is the price we pay for being responsible people, and that's as it should be. After all, think how patient our heavenly Father has been with us. So the next time you find yourselves drumming your fingers as you wait for quick resolutions to the challenges of family life, take a deep breath and ask God for patience. Be still before your Heavenly Father and trust His timetable: it's the peaceful way to live.

Waiting is an essential part of spiritual discipline. It can be the ultimate test of faith.

Anne Graham Lotz

No matter what we are going through, no matter how long the waiting for answers, of one thing we may be sure. God is faithful. He keeps His promises. What he starts, He finishes…including His perfect work in us.

Gloria Gaither

To receive the blessing we need, we must believe and keep on believing, and we must also wait and keep on waiting. We need to wait in prayer, wait with our Bibles open as we confess his promises, wait in joyful praise and worship of the God who will never forget our case, and wait as we continue serving others in his name.

Jim Cymbala

Now we exhort you, brethren, warn those who are unruly, comfort the fainthearted, uphold the weak, be patient with all.

1 Thessalonians 5:14 NKJV

Be gentle to everyone, able to teach, and patient.

2 Timothy 2:23 HOLMAN CSB

Love is patient; love is kind.

1 Corinthians 13:4 HOLMAN CSB

A patient spirit is better than a proud spirit.

Ecclesiastes 7:8 HOLMAN CSB

For More Thoughts About Patience, Please Turn to Page 164

FAMILY VALUES

We take seriously the Bible's instructions
to be patient.

We believe that patience is not idle waiting but
that it is an activity that requires us to watch
and wait for God to lead us.

Even when we don't understand the
circumstances that confront us, we strive to wait
patiently while serving the Lord.

CHECK ONE:	
YES	NO
_____	_____
_____	_____
_____	_____

A Family Prayer

Heavenly Father, let us wait quietly for You.
Let us live according to Your plan and according to
Your timetable. When we are hurried, slow us down.
When We become impatient with others, give us
empathy. Today, we want to be patient Christians,
Dear Lord, as we trust in You and
in Your master plan.
Amen

What We Can Do as a Family

_____

_____

_____

_____

_____

_____

_____

_____

_____

_____

_____

_____

_____

_____

_____

_____

_____

_____

SIGN ON!

_____

IF YOU AGREE TO THE ABOVE PLANS FOR OUR FAMILY. PLEASE SIGN YOUR NAME.

FORMING THE HABIT OF . . .

Monitoring the Media

*Pure and undefiled religion before our God
and Father is this: to look after orphans and
widows in their distress and to keep oneself
unstained by the world.*

James 1:27 HOLMAN CSB

I f you and your loved ones have acquired the bad habit of watching whatever happens to pop up on your family's TV screen, it's time to rethink the way you control your clicker. Most television networks (as well as the other forms of popular media) can be dangerous to your emotional and spiritual health.

The media is working around the clock in an attempt to rearrange your family's priorities in ways that are definitely not in your best interests. The media is trying to teach your family that physical appearance is all-important, that material possessions should be acquired at any cost, and that the world operates independently of God's laws. But guess what? Those messages are lies.

> It is impossible to please God doing things motivated by and produced by the flesh.
>
> Bill Bright

In the pursuit of profits, the media glamorizes violence, exploits suffering, and sensationalizes sex, all in the name of "ratings" (translated: "money").

So here's a question for you and your family: Will you control what appears on your TV screen, or will you be controlled by it? If you're willing to take complete control over the images that appear inside the four walls of your home, you'll be doing yourselves a king-sized favor. So forget the media hype, and pay attention to God. Stand up for Him and be counted, not just in church where it's relatively easy to be a Christian, but also when you're deciding what to watch. You owe it to your Creator . . . and you owe it to yourselves.

Every Christian is a contradiction to this old world. He crosses it at every point. He goes against the grain from beginning to end. From the day that he is born again until the day that he goes on to be with the Lord, he must stand against the current of a world always going the other way.

Vance Havner

A fish would never be happy living on land, because it was made for water. An eagle could never feel satisfied if it wasn't allowed to fly. You will never feel completely satisfied on earth, because you were made for more.

Rick Warren

Our fight is not against any physical enemy; it is against organizations and powers that are spiritual. We must struggle against sin all our lives, but we are assured we will win.

Corrie ten Boom

All those who look to draw their satisfaction from the wells of the world—pleasure, popularity, position, possessions, politics, power, prestige, finances, family, friends, fame, fortune, career, children, church, clubs, sports, sex, success, recognition, reputation, religion, education, entertainment, exercise, honors, health, hobbies—will soon be thirsty again!

Anne Graham Lotz

Now we have not received the spirit of the world, but the Spirit who is from God, in order to know what has been freely given to us by God.

1 Corinthians 2:12 HOLMAN CSB

No one should deceive himself. If anyone among you thinks he is wise in this age, he must become foolish so that he can become wise. For the wisdom of this world is foolishness with God, since it is written: He catches the wise in their craftiness.

1 Corinthians 3:18-19 HOLMAN CSB

Do not love the world or the things that belong to the world. If anyone loves the world, love for the Father is not in him.

1 John 2:15 HOLMAN CSB

Do not have other gods besides Me.

Exodus 20:3 HOLMAN CSB

For More Thoughts About Worldliness, Please Turn to Page 166

FAMILY VALUES

	CHECK ONE:	
	YES	NO

We will pay careful attention to the media images that are viewed in our home.

_____ _____

We will reject those images that are inappropriate for our family.

_____ _____

We will make God the cornerstone of our home, and we will watch and listen to programming that reinforces the principles set forth in God's Word.

_____ _____

We will be distrustful of media messages that are harmful to our family's spiritual or emotional health.

_____ _____

A Family Prayer

Dear Lord, we are imperfect human beings living in an imperfect world. Direct our paths far from the temptations and distractions of this world, and let us follow in the footsteps of Your Son today and forever.
Amen

What We Can Do as a Family

_____
_____
_____
_____
_____
_____
_____
_____
_____
_____
_____
_____
_____
_____
_____
_____
_____
_____
_____

SIGN ON!

IF YOU AGREE TO THE ABOVE PLANS FOR OUR FAMILY. PLEASE SIGN YOUR NAME.

FORMING THE HABIT OF . . .

(WHILE TRUSTING GOD MORE)

*Trust in the Lord with all your heart,
and do not rely on your own understanding;
think about Him in all your ways,
and He will guide you on the right paths.*

Proverbs 3:5-6 HOLMAN CSB

Because you and your family members have the ability to think, you also have the ability to worry. Even if you're very faithful Christians, you may be plagued by occasional periods of discouragement and doubt. Even though you trust God's promise of salvation—even though you sincerely believe in God's love and protection—you may find yourself upset by the countless details of everyday life. Jesus understood your concerns when He spoke the reassuring words found in the 6th chapter of Matthew.

"Therefore I say to you, do not worry about your life, what you will eat or what you will drink; nor about your body, what you will put on. Is not life more than food and the body more than clothing? Look at the birds of the air, for they neither sow nor reap nor gather into barns; yet your heavenly Father feeds them. Are you not of more value than they? Which of you by worrying can add one cubit to his stature? . . . Therefore do not worry about tomorrow, for tomorrow will worry about its own things. Sufficient for the day is its own trouble." (vv. 25-27, 34 NKJV)

> Never imagine that you can be a loser by trusting in God.
>
> C. H. Spurgeon

Where is the best place to take your worries? Take them to God. Take your troubles to Him; take your fears to Him; take your doubts to Him; take your weaknesses to Him; take your sorrows to Him . . . and leave them all there. Seek protection from the One who offers you eternal salvation—build your spiritual house upon the Rock that cannot be moved.

Perhaps you or your loved ones are concerned about the future, or about your relationships, or about your finances. Or perhaps you are simply "worriers" by nature. If so, choose to make Matthew 6 a regular part of your daily Bible readings. This beautiful passage will remind you that God still sits in His heaven and that you are His beloved children. Then, perhaps, you will worry a little less and trust God a little more, and that's as it should be because God is trustworthy…and you are protected.

For each of us, the time is surely coming when we shall have nothing but God. Health and wealth and friends and hiding places will all be swept away, and we shall have only God. To the man of pseudo faith this is a terrifying thought, but to a man of real faith, it is one of the most comforting thoughts the heart can entertain.

A. W. Tozer

As God's children, we are the recipients of lavish love—a love that motivates us to keep trusting even when we have no idea what God is doing.

Beth Moore

For the eyes of the Lord range throughout the earth to show Himself strong for those whose hearts are completely His.

2 Chronicles 16:9 HOLMAN CSB

He granted their request because they trusted in Him.

1 Chronicles 5:20 HOLMAN CSB

Let us hold fast the confession of our hope without wavering, for He who promised is faithful.

Hebrews 10:23 NKJV

The one who understands a matter finds success, and the one who trusts in the Lord will be happy.

Proverbs 16:20 HOLMAN CSB

For More Thoughts About Worry, Please Turn to Page 168

FAMILY VALUES

	CHECK ONE:	
	YES	NO

We will trust God in every season of life,
in good times and hard times.

_____ _____

We will use faith as an antidote to worry.

_____ _____

We will remember that God has been
trustworthy in the past, so we will trust Him to
protect us today.

_____ _____

We will trust God's Word, and we will expect
Him to fulfill His promises.

_____ _____

A Family Prayer

*Lord, when we trust in things of this earth, we will be
disappointed. But, when we put our faith in You,
we are secure. You are our rock and our shield.
Upon Your firm foundation, we will build our lives.
When we are worried, Lord, let us trust in You.
You will love us and protect us, and You will share
Your boundless grace today, tomorrow, and forever.*
Amen

What We Can Do as a Family

_____

_____

_____

_____

_____

_____

_____

_____

_____

_____

_____

_____

_____

_____

_____

_____

_____

_____

SIGN ON!

IF YOU AGREE TO THE ABOVE PLANS FOR OUR FAMILY, PLEASE SIGN YOUR NAME.

FORMING THE HABIT OF . . .

Discipline

No discipline seems enjoyable at the time, but painful. Later on, however, it yields the fruit of peace and righteousness to those who have been trained by it.

Hebrews 12:11 HOLMAN CSB

God's Word reminds us again and again that our Creator expects us to lead disciplined lives. God doesn't reward laziness, misbehavior, or apathy. To the contrary, He expects us to behave with dignity and discipline. But ours is a world in which dignity and discipline are often in short supply.

We live in a world where undisciplined behavior is often glorified and indifference is often glamorized. But God has other plans. God gives us talents, and He expects us to use them. Of course, it's not always easy to cultivate these talents. Sometimes, we must invest countless hours (or, in some cases, many years) honing our skills. And that's perfectly okay with God, because He understands that self-discipline is a blessing, not a burden.

> Discipline is training that develops and corrects.
>
> Charles Stanley

Proverbs 23:12 advises: "Apply your heart to discipline and your ears to words of knowledge" (NASB). And, 2 Peter 1:5-6 teaches, "make every effort to supplement your faith with goodness, goodness with knowledge, knowledge with self-control, self-control with endurance, endurance with godliness" (HOLMAN CSB). Thus, God's Word is clear: we must develop the habit of self-discipline . . . or suffer the consequences.

When we pause to consider how much work needs to be done, we realize that self-discipline is not simply a proven way to get ahead, it's also an integral part of God's plan for our lives. If we genuinely seek to be faithful stewards of our time, our talents, and our resources, we must adopt a disciplined approach to life. Otherwise, our talents are wasted and our resources are squandered.

Life's greatest rewards seldom fall into our laps; to the contrary, our greatest accomplishments usually require work, perseverance, and discipline. May we, as disciplined believers, be willing to work the rewards we so earnestly desire.

The Bible calls for discipline and a recognition of authority. Children must learn this at home.

Billy Graham

God cannot build character without our cooperation. If we resist Him, then He chastens us into submission. But, if we submit to Him, then He can accomplish His work. He is not satisfied with a halfway job. God wants a perfect work; He wants a finished product that is mature and complete.

Warren Wiersbe

As we seek to become disciples of Jesus Christ, we should never forget that the word disciple is directly related to the word discipline. To be a disciple of the Lord Jesus Christ is to know his discipline.

Dennis Swanberg

The one who follows instruction is on the path to life, but the one who rejects correction goes astray.

Proverbs 10:17 HOLMAN CSB

For this very reason, make every effort to supplement your faith with goodness, goodness with knowledge, knowledge with self-control, self-control with endurance, endurance with godliness.

2 Peter 1:5-6 HOLMAN CSB

I discipline my body and bring it under strict control, so that after preaching to others, I myself will not be disqualified.

1 Corinthians 9:27 HOLMAN CSB

Therefore by their fruits you will know them.

Matthew 7:20 NKJV

For More Thoughts About Self-Discipline, Please Turn to Page 170

FAMILY VALUES

	CHECK ONE:	
	YES	NO

We value the rewards of a disciplined lifestyle. _____ _____

We understand the importance of disciplining
ourselves emotionally, mentally, spiritually,
and physically. _____ _____

We believe that when we work hard, our work
is usually rewarded. _____ _____

A Family Prayer

Dear Lord, we want to be disciplined believers.
Let us use our time wisely, let us obey
Your commandments faithfully, and let us worship
You joyfully, today and every day.
Amen

What We Can Do as a Family

_____

_____

_____

_____

_____

_____

_____

_____

_____

_____

_____

_____

_____

_____

_____

_____

_____

_____

SIGN ON!

IF YOU AGREE TO THE ABOVE PLANS FOR OUR FAMILY, PLEASE SIGN YOUR NAME.

FORMING THE HABIT OF . . .

Living

Purposefully

For it is God who is working among you
both the willing and the working
for His good purpose.

Philippians 2:13 HOLMAN CSB

L ife is best lived on purpose, not by accident, so the sooner we acquire the habit of living purposefully, the better. But God's purposes aren't always clear to us. Sometimes we wander aimlessly in a wilderness of our own making. And sometimes, we struggle mightily against God in a vain effort to find success and happiness through our own means, not His.

Whenever we struggle against God's plans, we suffer. When we resist God's calling, our efforts bear little fruit. Our best strategy, therefore, is to seek God's wisdom and to follow Him wherever He chooses to lead. When we do so, we are blessed.

When we align ourselves with God's purposes, we avail ourselves of His power and His peace. But how can we know precisely what God's intentions are? The answer, of course, is that even the most well-intentioned believers face periods of uncertainty and doubt about the direction of their lives. So, too, will you.

> It's incredible to realize that what we do each day has meaning in the big picture of God's plan.
>
> Bill Hybels

When you or your loved ones arrive at one of life's inevitable crossroads, that is precisely the moment when you should turn your thoughts and prayers toward God. When you do, He will make Himself known to you in a time and manner of His choosing.

Are you and your family members earnestly seeking to discern God's purpose for your lives? If so, remember these important facts: 1. God has a plan for your lives; 2. If you seek that plan sincerely and prayerfully, you will find it; 3. When you discover God's purpose for your lives, you will experience abundance, peace, joy, and power—God's power. And that's the only kind of power that really matters.

If you want purpose and meaning and satisfaction and fulfillment and peace and hope and joy and abundant life that lasts forever, look to Jesus.

Anne Graham Lotz

Yesterday is just experience but tomorrow is glistening with purpose—and today is the channel leading from one to the other.

Barbara Johnson

It is important to set goals because if you do not have a plan, a goal, a direction, a purpose, and a focus, you are not going to accomplish anything for the glory of God.

Bill Bright

We aren't just thrown on this earth like dice tossed across a table. We are lovingly placed here for a purpose.

Charles Swindoll

We know that all things work together for the good of those who love God: those who are called according to His purpose.

Romans 8:28 HOLMAN CSB

I will instruct you and show you the way to go; with My eye on you, I will give counsel.

Psalm 32:8 HOLMAN CSB

You reveal the path of life to me; in Your presence is abundant joy; in Your right hand are eternal pleasures.

Psalm 16:11 HOLMAN CSB

Commit your activities to the Lord and your plans will be achieved.

Proverbs 16:3 HOLMAN CSB

For More Thoughts About Living Purposefully,
Please Turn to Page 172

FAMILY VALUES

	CHECK ONE:	
	YES	NO

We will seek to discover God's unfolding
purpose for our life.

_____ _____

We will consult God on matters great and small.

_____ _____

We will pray about our plans for the future.

_____ _____

We will remain open to the opportunities and
challenges that God places before us.

_____ _____

A Family Prayer

Dear Lord, we seek to live meaningful lives;
we will turn to You to find that meaning. We will
study Your Word, we will obey Your commandments,
we will trust Your providence, and we will honor
Your Son. Give us Your blessings, Father,
and lead our family along a path that is pleasing to
You, today, tomorrow, and forever.
Amen

What We Can Do as a Family

SIGN ON!

IF YOU AGREE TO THE ABOVE PLANS FOR OUR FAMILY, PLEASE SIGN YOUR NAME.

More Thoughts About . . .

OBEDIENCE

Christ reigns in his church as shepherd-king. He has supremacy, but it is the superiority of a wise and tender shepherd over his needy and loving flock. He commands and receives obedience, but it is willing obedience of well-cared-for-sheep, offered joyfully to their beloved Shepherd, whose voice they know so well. He rules by the force of love and the energy of goodness.

C. H. Spurgeon

The strength and happiness of a man consists in finding out the way in which God is going, and going that way too.

Henry Ward Beecher

Mary could not have dreamed all that would result from her faithful obedience. Likewise, you cannot possibly imagine all that God has in store for you when you trust him.

Henry Blackaby

Obedience is the road to freedom, humility the road to pleasure, unity the road to personality.

C. S. Lewis

Let us never suppose that obedience is impossible or that holiness is meant only for a select few. Our Shepherd leads us in paths of righteousness—not for our name's sake but for His.

Elisabeth Elliot

When you suffer and lose, that does not mean you are being disobedient to God. In fact, it might mean you're right in the center of His will. The path of obedience is often marked by times of suffering and loss.

Charles Swindoll

I don't always like His decisions, but when I choose to obey Him, the act of obedience still "counts" with Him even if I'm not thrilled about it.

Beth Moore

Trials and sufferings teach us to obey the Lord by faith, and we soon learn that obedience pays off in joyful ways.

Bill Bright

Let your fellowship with the Father and with the Lord Jesus Christ have as its one aim and object a life of quiet, determined, unquestioning obedience.

Andrew Murray

True faith commits us to obedience.

A. W. Tozer

PRAYER

It is well said that neglected prayer is the birth-place of all evil.

C. H. Spurgeon

Obedience is the master key to effective prayer.

Billy Graham

Prayer guards hearts and minds and causes God to bring peace out of chaos.

Beth Moore

Allow your dreams a place in your prayers and plans. God-given dreams can help you move into the future He is preparing for you.

Barbara Johnson

Those who know God the best are the richest and most powerful in prayer. Little acquaintance with God, and strangeness and coldness to Him, make prayer a rare and feeble thing.

E. M. Bounds

The Christian on his knees sees more than the philosopher on tiptoe.

D. L. Moody

My soul, hearken to the voice of your God. He is always ready
to speak with you when you are prepared to hear. If there is any
slowness to commune, it is not on His part but altogether on
your own. He stands at the door and knocks, and if His people
will only open, He rejoices to enter.

C. H. Spurgeon

God delights in the prayers of His children—prayers that express our love for Him, prayers that share our deepest burdens with Him.

Billy Graham

Pour out your heart to God and tell Him how you feel. Be real,
be honest, and when you get it all out, you'll start to feel the
gradual covering of God's comforting presence.

Bill Hybels

On our knees we are the most powerful force on earth.

Billy Graham

FORGIVENESS

As you have received the mercy of God by the forgiveness of sin and the promise of eternal life, thus you must show mercy.

Billy Graham

Only the truly forgiven are truly forgiving.

C. S. Lewis

Our relationships with other people are of primary importance to God. Because God is love, He cannot tolerate any unforgiveness or hardness in us toward any individual.

Catherine Marshall

Forgiveness is not an emotion. Forgiveness is an act of the will, and the will can function regardless of the temperature of the heart.

Corrie ten Boom

Revenge is the raging fire that consumes the arsonist.

Max Lucado

The more you practice the art of forgiving, the quicker you'll master the art of living.

Marie T. Freeman

Our forgiveness toward others should flow from a realization and appreciation of God's forgiveness toward us.

Franklin Graham

To hold on to hate and resentments is to throw a monkey wrench into the machinery of life.

E. Stanley Jones

I firmly believe a great many prayers are not answered because we are not willing to forgive someone.

D. L. Moody

It is better to forgive and forget than to resent and remember.

Barbara Johnson

SERVICE

God wants us to serve Him with a willing spirit, one that would choose no other way.

Beth Moore

No life can surpass that of a man who quietly continues to serve God in the place where providence has placed him.

C. H. Spurgeon

Have thy tools ready; God will find thee work.

Charles Kingsley

In the very place where God has put us, whatever its limitations, whatever kind of work it may be, we may indeed serve the Lord Christ.

Elisabeth Elliot

If you love, service will be the logical and natural outcome.

Charles Stanley

Holy service in constant fellowship with God is heaven below.

C. H. Spurgeon

A Christian is a perfectly free lord of all, subject to none.
A Christian is a perfectly dutiful servant of all, subject to all.

Martin Luther

If doing a good act in public will excite others to do more good, then "Let your Light shine to all." Miss no opportunity to do good.

John Wesley

You can judge how far you have risen
in the scale of life by asking one question:
How wisely and how deeply do I care?
To be Christianized is to be sensitized.
Christians are people who care.

E. Stanley Jones

We are only fully alive when we're helping others.

Rick Warren

PRAISE AND THANKSGIVING

Words fail to express my love for this holy Book, my gratitude for its author, for His love and goodness. How shall I thank him for it?

Lottie Moon

A child of God should be a visible beatitude for joy and a living doxology for gratitude.

C. H. Spurgeon

The time for universal praise is sure to come some day. Let us begin to do our part now.

Hannah Whitall Smith

Praise reestablishes the proper chain of command; we recognize that the King is on the throne and that he has saved his people.

Max Lucado

Nothing we do is more powerful or more life-changing than praising God.

Stormie Omartian

Praise is the highest occupation of any being.

Max Lucado

Holy, holy, holy! Lord God Almighty! All Thy works shall praise Thy name in earth, and sky, and sea.

Reginald Heber

Our God is the sovereign Creator of the universe! He loves us as His own children and has provided every good thing we have; He is worthy of our praise every moment.

Shirley Dobson

The best moment to praise God is always the present one.

Marie T. Freeman

This is my story, this is my song, praising my Savior, all the day long.

Fanny Crosby

LOVE

Love must be supported and fed and protected, just like a little infant who is growing up at home.

James Dobson

Beware that you are not swallowed up in books! An ounce of love is worth a pound of knowledge.

John Wesley

Brotherly love is still the distinguishing badge of every true Christian.

Matthew Henry

Forgiveness is the final form of love.

Reinhold Niebuhr

How do you spell love? When you reach the point where the happiness, security, and development of another person is as much of a driving force to you as your own happiness, security, and development, then you have a mature love. True love is spelled G-I-V-E. It is not based on what you can get, but rooted in what you can give to the other person.

Josh McDowell

The truth of the Gospel is intended to free us to love God and others with our whole heart.

John Eldredge

Truth becomes hard if it is not softened by love, and love becomes soft if not strengthened by truth.

E. Stanley Jones

Love is not measured by what it gets,
but by what it costs.

Oswald Chambers

It is important to know that you have to work to keep love alive; you have to protect it and maintain it, just like you would a delicate flower.

James Dobson

WORSHIP

I am of the opinion that we should not be concerned about working for God until we have learned the meaning and delight of worshipping Him.

A. W. Tozer

To worship Him in truth means to worship Him honestly, without hypocrisy, standing open and transparent before Him.

Anne Graham Lotz

Each time, before you intercede, be quiet first and worship God in His glory. Think of what He can do and how He delights to hear the prayers of His redeemed people. Think of your place and privilege in Christ, and expect great things!

Andrew Murray

Worship is spiritual. Our worship must be more than just outward expression, it must also take place in our spirits.

Franklin Graham

Inside the human heart is an undeniable, spiritual instinct to commune with its Creator.

Jim Cymbala

Worship is a daunting task. Each worships differently. But each should worship.

Max Lucado

God asks that we worship Him with our concentrated minds as well as with our wills and emotions. A divided and scattered mind is not effective.

Catherine Marshall

Worship is your spirit responding to God's Spirit.

Rick Warren

It is impossible to worship God and remain unchanged.

Henry Blackaby

Praise Him! Praise Him! Tell of His excellent greatness.
Praise Him! Praise Him! Ever in joyful song!

Fanny Crosby

ENCOURAGEMENT

Always stay connected to people and seek out things that bring you joy. Dream with abandon. Pray confidently.

Barbara Johnson

I can usually sense that a leading is from the Holy Spirit when it calls me to humble myself, to serve somebody, to encourage somebody, or to give something away. Very rarely will the evil one lead us to do those kind of things.

Bill Hybels

God grant that we may not hinder those who are battling their way slowly into the light.

Oswald Chambers

The truest help we can render an afflicted man is not to take his burden from him, but to call out his best energy, that he may be able to bear the burden himself.

Phillips Brooks

Encouragement starts at home, but it should never end there.

Marie T. Freeman

You can't light another's path without casting light on your own.

John Maxwell

If I am asked how we are to get rid of discouragements, I can only say, as I have had to say of so many other wrong spiritual habits, we must give them up. It is never worth while to argue against discouragement. There is only one argument that can meet it, and that is the argument of God.

Hannah Whitall Smith

A single word, if spoken in a friendly spirit, may be sufficient to turn one from dangerous error.

Fanny Crosby

It is helpful to remember the distinction between appreciation and affirmation. We appreciate what a person does, but we affirm who a person is.

Charles Swindoll

Sometimes one little spark of kindness is all it takes to reignite the light of hope in a heart that's blinded by pain.

Barbara Johnson

ATTITUDE

Attitude is more important than the past, than education, than money, than circumstances, than what people do or say. It is more important than appearance, giftedness, or skill.

Charles Swindoll

The mind is like a clock that is constantly running down. It has to be wound up daily with good thoughts.

Fulton J. Sheen

The difference between winning and losing is how we choose to react to disappointment.

Barbara Johnson

I have witnessed many attitudes make a positive turnaround through prayer.

John Maxwell

It's your choice: you can either count your blessings or recount your disappointments.

Jim Gallery

The Reference Point for the Christian is the Bible. All values, judgments, and attitudes must be gauged in relationship to this Reference Point.

Ruth Bell Graham

Attitude is the mind's paintbrush; it can color any situation.

Barbara Johnson

Life is 10% what happens to you and 90% how you respond to it.

Charles Swindoll

You've heard the saying, 'Life is what you make it.' That means we have a choice. We can choose to have a life full of frustration and fear, but we can just as easily choose one of joy and contentment.

Dennis Swanberg

All things being equal, attitude wins. All things not being equal, attitude sometimes still wins.

John Maxwell

JOYFUL CELEBRATION

Joy is the direct result of having God's perspective on our daily lives and the effect of loving our Lord enough to obey His commands and trust His promises.

Bill Bright

God knows everything. He can manage everything, and He loves us. Surely this is enough for a fullness of joy that is beyond words.

Hannah Whitall Smith

He wants us to have a faith that does not complain while waiting, but rejoices because we know our times are in His hands—nail-scarred hands that labor for our highest good.

Kay Arthur

A life of intimacy with God is characterized by joy.

Oswald Chambers

Our God is so wonderfully good, and lovely, and blessed in every way that the mere fact of belonging to Him is enough for an untellable fullness of joy!

Hannah Whitall Smith

God gives to us a heavenly gift called joy, radically different in quality from any natural joy.

Elisabeth Elliot

Our sense of joy, satisfaction, and fulfillment in life increases, no matter what the circumstances, if we are in the center of God's will.

Billy Graham

Where the soul is full of peace and joy, outward surroundings and circumstances are of comparatively little account.

Hannah Whitall Smiith

When we get rid of inner conflicts
and wrong attitudes toward life,
we will almost automatically
burst into joy.

E. Stanley Jones

Lord, I thank you for the promise of heaven and the unexpected moments when you touch my heartstrings with that longing for my eternal home.

Joni Eareckson Tada

PATIENCE

Waiting is the hardest kind of work, but God knows best, and we may joyfully leave all in His hands.

Lottie Moon

God is more patient with us than we are with ourselves.

Max Lucado

If God is diligent, surely we ought to be diligent in doing our duty to Him. Think how patient and diligent God has been to us!

Oswald Chambers

When I am dealing with an all-powerful, all-knowing God, I, as a mere mortal, must offer my petitions not only with persistence, but also with patience. Someday I'll know why.

Ruth Bell Graham

In the Bible, patience is not a passive acceptance of circumstances. It is a courageous perseverance in the face of suffering and difficulty.

Warren Wiersbe

The next time you're disappointed, don't panic. Don't give up. Just be patient and let God remind you he's still in control.

Max Lucado

Grass that is here today and gone tomorrow does not require much time to mature. A big oak tree that lasts for generations requires much more time to grow and mature. God is concerned about your life through eternity. Allow Him to take all the time He needs to shape you for His purposes. Larger assignments will require longer periods of preparation.

Henry Blackaby

When we read of the great Biblical leaders, we see that it was not uncommon for God to ask them to wait, not just a day or two, but for years, until God was ready for them to act.

Gloria Gaither

It is wise to wait because
God gives clear direction
only when we are willing to wait.

Charles Stanley

WORLDLINESS

The true Christian, though he is in revolt against the world's efforts to brainwash him, is no mere rebel for rebellion's sake. He dissents from the world because he knows that it cannot make good on its promises.

A. W. Tozer

Every day, I find countless opportunities to decide whether I will obey God and demonstrate my love for Him or try to please myself or the world system. God is waiting for my choices.

Bill Bright

Too many Christians have geared their program to please, to entertain, and to gain favor from this world. We are concerned with how much, instead of how little, like this age we can become.

Billy Graham

Tell me that you love the world, and I will tell you that love of the world is enmity to God.

C. H. Spurgeon

Aim at heaven and you will get earth thrown in; aim at earth and you will get neither.

C. S. Lewis

The Lord Jesus Christ is still praying for us. He wants us to be in the world but not of it.

Charles Stanley

The only ultimate disaster that can befall us, I have come to realize, is to feel ourselves to be home on earth.

Max Lucado

The person of the world loves himself; the Christian loves his God.

C. H. Spurgeon

Because the world is deceptive, it is dangerous. The world can even deceive God's own people and lead them into trouble.

Warren Wiersbe

The world's sewage system threatens to contaminate the stream of Christian thought. Is the world shaping your mind, or is Christ?

Billy Graham

WORRY

Worry is the senseless process of cluttering up tomorrow's opportunities with leftover problems from today.

Barbara Johnson

God is bigger than your problems. Whatever worries press upon you today, put them in God's hands and leave them there.

Billy Graham

We are not called to be burden-bearers, but cross-bearers and light-bearers. We must cast our burdens on the Lord.

Corrie ten Boom

This life of faith, then, consists in just this—being a child in the Father's house. Let the ways of childish confidence and freedom from care, which so please you and win your heart when you observe your own little ones, teach you what you should be in your attitude toward God.

Hannah Whitall Smith

Pray, and let God worry.

Martin Luther

Today is mine. Tomorrow is none of my business. If I peer anxiously into the fog of the future, I will strain my spiritual eyes so that I will not see clearly what is required of me now.

Elisabeth Elliott

Worry and anxiety are sand in the machinery of life; faith is the oil.

E. Stanley Jones

Today is the tomorrow we worried about yesterday.

Dennis Swanberg

Worries carry responsibilities that belong to God, not to you. Worry does not enable us to escape evil; it makes us unfit to cope with it when it comes.

Corrie ten Boom

I've read the last page of the Bible. It's all going to turn out all right.

Billy Graham

SELF-DISCIPLINE

Simply stated, self-discipline is obedience to God's Word and willingness to submit everything in life to His will, for His ultimate glory.

John MacArthur

If one examines the secret behind a championship football team, a magnificent orchestra, or a successful business, the principal ingredient is invariably discipline.

James Dobson

Obedience to God is our job. The results of that obedience are God's.

Elisabeth Elliot

Hoping for a good future without investing in today is like a farmer waiting for a crop without ever planting any seed.

John Maxwell

"They that sow bountifully shall reap also bountifully," is as true in spiritual things as in material.

Lottie Moon

As we make an offering of our work, we find the truth of a principle Jesus taught: Fulfillment is not a goal to achieve, but always the by-product of a sacrifice.

Elisabeth Elliot

Working in the vineyard, Working all the day, Never be discouraged, Only watch and pray.

Fanny Crosby

The world does not consider labor a blessing, therefore it flees and hates it, but the pious who fear the Lord labor with a ready and cheerful heart, for they know God's command, and they acknowledge His calling.

Martin Luther

You can't climb the ladder of life
with your hands in your pockets.

Barbara Johnson

The alternative to discipline is disaster.

Vance Havner

LIVING PURPOSEFULLY

Continually restate to yourself what the purpose of your life is.

Oswald Chambers

When God speaks to you through the Bible, prayer, circumstances, the church, or in some other way, he has a purpose in mind for your life.

Henry Blackaby and Claude King

Without God, life has no purpose, and without purpose, life has no meaning.

Rick Warren

Whatever purpose motivates your life, it must be something big enough and grand enough to make the investment worthwhile.

Warren Wiersbe

The worst thing that laziness does is rob a man of spiritual purpose.

Billy Graham

God wants to revolutionize our lives—by showing us how knowing Him can be the most powerful force to help us become all we want to be.

Bill Hybels

Their distress is due entirely to their deliberate determination to use themselves for a purpose other than God's.

Oswald Chambers

God is more concerned with the direction of your life than with its speed.

Marie T. Freeman

God specializes in things fresh and firsthand. His plans for you this year may outshine those of the past. He's prepared to fill your days with reasons to give Him praise.

Joni Eareckson Tada

Oh Lord, let me not live to be useless.

John Wesley

Read the Bible with Your Family in a Year

January

1 Genesis 1-2 Matthew 1	2 Genesis 3-5 Matthew 2	3 Genesis 6-8 Matthew 3	4 Genesis 9-11 Matthew 4
5 Genesis 12-14 Matthew 5:1-20	6 Genesis 15-17 Matthew 5:21-48	7 Genesis 18-19 Matthew 6:1-18	8 Genesis 20-21 Matthew 6:19-34
9 Genesis 22-25 Matthew 7	10 Genesis 26-27 Matthew 8:1-20	11 Genesis 28-29 Matthew 8:21-34	12 Genesis 30-31 Matthew 9:1-17
13 Genesis 32-33 Matthew 9:18-38	14 Genesis 34-35 Matthew 10:1-24	15 Genesis 36-38 Matthew 10:25-42	16 Genesis 39-40 Matthew 11
17 Genesis 41-42 Matthew 12:1-24	18 Genesis 43-44 Matthew 12:25-50	19 Genesis 45-46 Matthew 13:1-36	20 Genesis 47-48 Matthew 13:37-58
21 Genesis 49-50 Matthew 14	22 Exodus 1-3 Matthew 15:1-20	23 Exodus 4-6 Matthew 15:21-39	24 Exodus 7-9 Matthew 16
25 Exodus 10-12 Matthew 17	26 Exodus 13-14 Matthew 18:1-20	27 Exodus 15-16 Matthew 18:21-35	28 Exodus 17-18 Matthew 19
29 Exodus 19-20 Matthew 20:1-16	30 Exodus 21-22 Matthew 20:17-34	31 Exodus 23-24 Matthew 21:1-22	

Thoughts for the Month

FEBRUARY

1	2	3	4
Exodus 25-27 Matthew 21:23-46	Exodus 28-30 Matthew 22:1-22	Exodus 31-33 Matthew 22:23-46	Exodus 34-35 Matthew 23
5	6	7	8
Exodus 36-37 Matthew 24:1-28	Exodus 38-39 Matthew 24:29-51	Exodus 40 Matthew 25	Leviticus 1-2 Matthew 26:1-29
9	10	11	12
Leviticus 3-4 Matthew 26:30-56	Leviticus 5-6 Matthew 26:57-75	Leviticus 7-8 Matthew 27:1-26	Leviticus 9-10 Matthew 27:27-53
13	14	15	16
Leviticus 11-12 Matthew 27:54-66	Leviticus 13-14 Matthew 28	Leviticus 15-16 Mark 1:1-28	Leviticus 17-18 Mark 1:29-45
17	18	19	20
Leviticus 19-20 Mark 2	Leviticus 21-22 Mark 3:1-19	Leviticus 23-24 Mark 3:20-35	Leviticus 25 Mark 4:1-20
21	22	23	24
Leviticus 26-27 Mark 4:21-41	Numbers 1-2 Mark 5:1-19	Numbers 3-4 Mark 5:20-43	Numbers 5-6 Mark 6:1-12
25	26	27	28
Numbers 7-9 Mark 6:13-32	Numbers 10-12 Mark 6:33-56	Numbers 13-15 Mark 7:1-13	Numbers 16-18 Mark 7:14-37

THOUGHTS FOR THE MONTH

MARCH

1 Numbers 19-21 Mark 8:1-13	2 Numbers 22-24 Mark 8:14-38	3 Numbers 25-27 Mark 9:1-29	4 Numbers 28-30 Mark 9:30-50
5 Numbers 31-33 Mark 10:1-31	6 Numbers 34-36 Mark 10:32-52	7 Deuteronomy 1-3 Mark 11:1-19	8 Deuteronomy 4-6 Mark 11:20-33
9 Deuteronomy 7-9 Mark 12:1-28	10 Deuteronomy 10-12 Mark 12:29-44	11 Deuteronomy 13-15 Mark 13	12 Deuteronomy 16-18 Mark 14:1-9
13 Deuteronomy 19-21 Mark 14:10-36	14 Deuteronomy 22-24 Mark 14:37-72	15 Deuteronomy 25-27 Mark 15:1-26	16 Deuteronomy 28-30 Mark 15:27-47
17 Deuteronomy 31-32 Mark 16	18 Deuteronomy 33-34 Luke 1:1-38	19 Joshua 1-3 Luke 1:39-80	20 Joshua 4-6 Luke 2:1-24
21 Joshua 7-9 Luke 2:25-52	22 Joshua 10-12 Luke 3:1-18	23 Joshua 13-15 Luke 3:19-38	24 Joshua 16-18 Luke 4:1-13
25 Joshua 19-21 Luke 4:14-30	26 Joshua 22-24 Luke 4:31-44	27 Judges 1-2 Luke 5:1-16	28 Judges 3-5 Luke 5:17-39
29 Judges 6-8 Luke 6:1-18	30 Judges 9-11 Luke 6:19-49	31 Judges 12-13 Luke 7:1-28	

THOUGHTS FOR THE MONTH

APRIL

1 Judges 14-15 Luke 7:29-50	2 Judges 16-17 Luke 8:1-21	3 Judges 18-19 Luke 8:22-40	4 Judges 20-21 Luke 8:41-56
5 Ruth 1-2 Luke 9:1-17	6 Ruth 3-4 Luke 9:18-36	7 1 Samuel 1-3 Luke 9:37-62	8 1 Samuel 4-6 Luke 10:1-24
9 1 Samuel 7-9 Luke 10:25-42	10 1 Samuel 10-12 Luke 11:1-36	11 1 Samuel 13-15 Luke 11:37-54	12 1 Samuel 16-18 Luke 12:1-40
13 1 Samuel 19-21 Luke 12:41-59	14 1 Samuel 22-24 Luke 13:1-21	15 1 Samuel 25-27 Luke 13:22-35	16 1 Samuel 28-29 Luke 14:1-14
17 1 Samuel 30-31 Luke 14:15-35	18 2 Samuel 1-3 Luke 15	19 2 Samuel 4-6 Luke 16:1-13	20 2 Samuel 7-9 Luke 16:14-31
21 2 Samuel 10-12 Luke 17:1-19	22 2 Samuel 13-15 Luke 17:20-37	23 2 Samuel 16-18 Luke 18:1-17	24 2 Samuel 19-21 Luke 18:18-43
25 2 Samuel 22-24 Luke 19:1-27	26 1 Kings 1-2 Luke 19:28-48	27 1 Kings 3-4 Luke 20:1-18	28 1 Kings 5-6 Luke 20:19-47
29 1 Kings 7-8 Luke 21	30 1 Kings 9-10 Luke 22:1-22		

THOUGHTS FOR THE MONTH

May

1 1 Kings 11-12 Luke 22:23-53	2 1 Kings 13-14 Luke 22:54-71	3 1 Kings 15-16 Luke 23:1-25	4 1 Kings 17-18 Luke 23:26-56
5 1 Kings 19-20 Luke 24:1-20	6 1 Kings 21-22 Luke 24:21-36	7 2 Kings 1-2 Luke 24:37-53	8 2 Kings 3-5 John 1:1-28
9 2 Kings 6-8 John 1:29-51	10 2 Kings 9-11 John 2	11 2 Kings 12-13 John 3:1-21	12 2 Kings 14-16 John 3:22-36
13 2 Kings 17-19 John 4:1-30	14 2 Kings 20-21 John 4:31-54	15 2 Kings 22-23 John 5:1-18	16 2 Kings 24-25 John 5:19-47
17 1 Chronicles 1-3 John 6:1-21	18 1 Chronicles 4-6 John 6:22-40	19 1 Chronicles 7-9 John 6:41-58	20 1 Chronicles 10-12 John 6:59-71
21 1 Chronicles 13-15 John 7:1-32	22 1 Chronicles 16-18 John 7:33-53	23 1 Chronicles 19-21 John 8:1-30	24 1 Chronicles 22-24 John 8:31-59
25 1 Chronicles 25-26 John 9	26 1 Chronicles 27-29 John 10:1-18	27 2 Chronicles 1-2 John 10:19-42	28 2 Chronicles 3-5 John 11:1-29
29 2 Chronicles 6-8 John 11:30-57	30 2 Chronicles 9-11 John 12:1-16	31 2 Chronicles 12-14 John 12:17-36	

Thoughts for the Month

JUNE

1 2 Chronicles 15-17 John 12:37-50	2 2 Chronicles 18-19 John 13:1-20	3 2 Chronicles 20-21 John 13:21-38	4 2 Chronicles 22-23 John 14
5 2 Chronicles 24-25 John 15	6 2 Chronicles 26-27 John 16	7 2 Chronicles 28-29 John 17	8 2 Chronicles 30-31 John 18:1-19
9 2 Chronicles 32-34 John 18:20-40	10 2 Chronicles 35-36 John 19:1-28	11 Ezra 1-3 John 19:29-42	12 Ezra 4-6 John 20
13 Ezra 7-8 John 21	14 Ezra 9-10 Acts 1	15 Nehemiah 1-2 Acts 2	16 Nehemiah 3-5 Acts 3
17 Nehemiah 6-8 Acts 4	18 Nehemiah 9-10 Acts 5	19 Nehemiah 11-13 Acts 6	20 Esther 1-3 Acts 7:1-39
21 Esther 4-5 Acts 7:40-60	22 Esther 6-7 Acts 8:1-13	23 Esther 8-10 Acts 8:14-40	24 Job 1-3 Acts 9:1-22
25 Job 4-5 Acts 9:23-43	26 Job 6-7 Acts 10:1-23	27 Job 8-9 Acts 10:24-48	28 Job 10-11 Acts 11:1-18
29 Job 12-14 Acts 11:19-30	30 Job 15-17 Acts 12		

THOUGHTS FOR THE MONTH

JULY

1 Job 18-20 Acts 13:1-12	2 Job 21-23 Acts 13:13-31	3 Job 24-26 Acts 13:32-52	4 Job 27-29 Acts 14
5 Job 30-32 Acts 15:1-21	6 Job 33-34 Acts 15:22-41	7 Job 35-36 Acts 16:1-22	8 Job 37-38 Acts 16:23-40
9 Job 39-40 Acts 17:1-15	10 Job 41-42 Acts 17:16-34	11 Psalms 1-3 Acts 18	12 Psalms 4-6 Acts 19
13 Psalms 7-8 Acts 20	14 Psalms 9-11 Acts 21:1-17	15 Psalms 12-14 Acts 21:18-40	16 Psalms 15-17 Acts 22:1-11
17 Psalms 18 Acts 22:12-30	18 Psalms 19-20 Acts 23:1-11	19 Psalms 21-22 Acts 23:12-35	20 Psalms 23-25 Acts 24
21 Psalms 26-27 Acts 25	22 Psalms 28-29 Acts 26	23 Psalms 30-33 Acts 27:1-18	24 Psalms 34-35 Acts 27:19-44
25 Psalms 36-38 Acts 28:1-10	26 Psalms 39-41 Acts 28:11-31	27 Psalms 42-44 Romans 1	28 Psalms 45-46 Romans 2
29 Psalms 47-48 Romans 3	30 Psalms 49-50 Romans 4	31 Psalms 51-53 Romans 5	

THOUGHTS FOR THE MONTH

AUGUST

1 Psalms 54-57 Romans 6	2 Psalms 58-60 Romans 7	3 Psalms 61-64 Romans 8:1-21	4 Psalms 65-66 Romans 8:22-39
5 Psalms 67-68 Romans 9:1-16	6 Psalms 69 Romans 9:17-33	7 Psalms 70-72 Romans 10	8 Psalms 73-74 Romans 11:1-21
9 Psalms 75-77 Romans 11:22-36	10 Psalms 78 Romans 12	11 Psalms 79-81 Romans 13	12 Psalms 82-85 Romans 14
13 Psalms 86-88 Romans 15:1-13	14 Psalms 89 Romans 15:14-21	15 Psalms 90-93 Romans 15:22-33	16 Psalms 94-97 Romans 16
17 Psalms 98-100 1 Corinthians 1	18 Psalms 101-103 1 Corinthians 2	19 Psalms 104-105 1 Corinthians 3	20 Psalms 106 1 Corinthians 4
21 Psalms 107-109 1 Corinthians 5	22 Psalms 110-113 1 Corinthians 6	23 Psalms 114-118 1 Corinthians 7	24 Psalms 119:1-72 1 Corinthians 8
25 Psalms 119:73-176 1 Corinthians 9	26 Psalms 120-123 1 Corinthians 10:1-13	27 Psalms 124-127 1 Corinthians 10:14-33	28 Psalms 128-132 1 Corinthians 11:1-18
29 Psalms 133-135 1 Corinthians 11:19-34	30 Psalms 136-138 1 Corinthians 12:1-18	31 Psalms 139 1 Corinthians 12:19-31	

THOUGHTS FOR THE MONTH

September

1 Psalms 140-142 1 Corinthians 13	2 Psalms 143-145 1 Corinthians 14:1-19	3 Psalms 146-147 1 Corinthians 14:20-40	4 Psalms 148-150 1 Corinthians 15:1-11
5 Proverbs 1 1 Corinthians 15:12-25	6 Proverbs 2-3 1 Corinthians 15:26-58	7 Proverbs 4-5 1 Corinthians 16	8 Proverbs 6-7 2 Corinthians 1
9 Proverbs 8-9 2 Corinthians 2	10 Proverbs 10-11 2 Corinthians 3	11 Proverbs 12-13 2 Corinthians 4	12 Proverbs 14-15 2 Corinthians 5
13 Proverbs 16-17 2 Corinthians 6	14 Proverbs 18-19 2 Corinthians 7-8	15 Proverbs 20-21 2 Corinthians 9	16 Proverbs 22-23 2 Corinthians 10
17 Proverbs 24-25 2 Corinthians 11:1-11	18 Proverbs 26-27 2 Corinthians 11:12-33	19 Proverbs 28-29 2 Corinthians 12	20 Proverbs 30-31 2 Corinthians 13
21 Ecclesiastes 1-3 Galatians 1	22 Ecclesiastes 4-6 Galatians 2	23 Ecclesiastes 7-8 Galatians 3	24 Ecclesiastes 9-12 Galatians 4
25 Song of Solomon 1-4 Galatians 5	26 Song of Solomon 5-8 Galatians 6	27 Isaiah 1-2 Ephesians 1	28 Isaiah 3-4 Ephesians 2
29 Isaiah 5-6 Ephesians 3	30 Isaiah 7-8 Ephesians 4		

Thoughts for the Month

October

1 Isaiah 9-10 Ephesians 5	2 Isaiah 11-12 Ephesians 6	3 Isaiah 13-14 Philippians 1	4 Isaiah 15-16 Philippians 2
5 Isaiah 17-19 Philippians 3	6 Isaiah 20-22 Philippians 4	7 Isaiah 23-25 Colossians 1	8 Isaiah 26-27 Colossians 2
9 Isaiah 28-29 Colossians 3	10 Isaiah 30-31 Colossians 4	11 Isaiah 32-33 1 Thessalonians 1	12 Isaiah 34-35 1 Thessalonians 2
13 Isaiah 36-37 1 Thessalonians 3	14 Isaiah 38-39 1 Thessalonians 4	15 Isaiah 40-42 1 Thessalonians 5	16 Isaiah 43-45 2 Thessalonians 1
17 Isaiah 46-48 2 Thessalonians 2	18 Isaiah 49-51 2 Thessalonians 3	19 Isaiah 52-54 1 Timothy 1	20 Isaiah 55-57 1 Timothy 2
21 Isaiah 58-60 1 Timothy 3	22 Isaiah 61-63 1 Timothy 4	23 Isaiah 64-66 1 Timothy 5	24 Jeremiah 1-3 1 Timothy 6
25 Jeremiah 4-6 2 Timothy 1	26 Jeremiah 7-9 2 Timothy 2	27 Jeremiah 10-12 2 Timothy 3	28 Jeremiah 13-15 2 Timothy 4
29 Jeremiah 16-18 Titus 1	30 Jeremiah 19-20 Titus 2	31 Jeremiah 21-22 Titus 3	

Thoughts for the Month

November

1 Jeremiah 23-24 Philemon	2 Jeremiah 25-27 Hebrews 1	3 Jeremiah 28-30 Hebrews 2	4 Jeremiah 31-32 Hebrews 3
5 Jeremiah 33-35 Hebrews 4	6 Jeremiah 36-38 Hebrews 5	7 Jeremiah 39-41 Hebrews 6	8 Jeremiah 42-44 Hebrews 7
9 Jeremiah 45-47 Hebrews 8	10 Jeremiah 48-49 Hebrews 9	11 Jeremiah 50 Hebrews 10:1-22	12 Jeremiah 51 Hebrews 10:23-39
13 Jeremiah 52 Hebrews 11:1-16	14 Lamentations 1-2 Hebrews 11:17-40	15 Lamentations 3-5 Hebrews 12:1-13	16 Ezekiel 1-2 Hebrews 12:14-29
17 Ezekiel 3-5 Hebrews 13	18 Ezekiel 6-7 James 1	19 Ezekiel 8-10 James 2	20 Ezekiel 11-13 James 3
21 Ezekiel 14-16 James 4	22 Ezekiel 17-18 James 5	23 Ezekiel 19-20 1 Peter 1	24 Ezekiel 21-22 1 Peter 2
25 Ezekiel 23-24 1 Peter 3	26 Ezekiel 25-27 1 Peter 4	27 Ezekiel 28-30 1 Peter 5	28 Ezekiel 31-33 2 Peter 1
29 Ezekiel 34-36 2 Peter 2	30 Ezekiel 37-39 2 Peter 3		

Thoughts for the Month

December

1	2	3	4
Ezekiel 40-41	Ezekiel 42-44	Ezekiel 45-46	Ezekiel 47-48
1 John 1	1 John 2	1 John 3	1 John 4
5	6	7	8
Daniel 1-2	Daniel 3-4	Daniel 5-6	Daniel 7-8
1 John 5	2 John	3 John	Jude
9	10	11	12
Daniel 9-10	Daniel 11-12	Hosea 1-3	Hosea 4-7
Revelation 1	Revelation 2	Revelation 3	Revelation 4
13	14	15	16
Hosea 8-11	Hosea 12-14	Joel 1-3	Amos 1-4
Revelation 5	Revelation 6	Revelation 7	Revelation 8
17	18	19	20
Amos 5-9	Obadiah	Jonah 1-4	Micah 1-3
Revelation 9	Revelation 10	Revelation 11	Revelation 12
21	22	23	24
Micah 4-5	Micah 6-7	Nahum 1-3	Habakkuk 1-3
Revelation 13	Revelation 14	Revelation 15	Revelation 16
25	26	27	28
Zephaniah 1-3	Haggai 1-2	Zechariah 1-4	Zechariah 5-8
Revelation 17	Revelation 18	Revelation 19	Revelation 20
29	30	31	
Zechariah 9-11	Zechariah 12-14	Malachi 1-4	
Revelation 21	Revelation 22:1-8	Revelation 22:9-21	

Thoughts for the Month

READ THE BIBLE IN 52 WEEKS

Week 1	Week 2	Week 3
Genesis 1-18	Genesis 19-35	Genesis 36-50
Matthew 1-7	Matthew 8-10	Matthew 11-14

Week 4	Week 5	Week 6
Exodus 1-18	Exodus 19-35	Exodus 36-Leviticus 8
Matthew 15-19	Matthew 20-23	Matthew 24-27

Week 7	Week 8	Week 9
Leviticus 9-22	Leviticus 23-Numbers 9	Numbers 10-30
Matthew 28-Mark 4	Mark 5-6	Mark 7-9

Week 10	Week 11	Week 12
Numbers 31-Deuteronomy 15	Deuteronomy 16-34	Joshua 1-21
Mark 10-13	Mark 14-16	Luke 1-5

Week 13	Week 14	Week 15
Joshua 22-Judges 15	Judges 16-1 Samuel 6	1 Samuel 7-1 Samuel 27
Luke 6-8	Luke 9-11	Luke 12-14

Week 16	Week 17	Week 18
1 Samuel 28-2 Samuel 15	2 Samuel 16-1 Kings 8	1 Kings 9-2 Kings 2
Luke 15-17	Luke 18-21	Luke 22-24

Week 19	Week 20	Week 21
2 Kings 3-2 Kings 20	2 Kings 21-1 Chronicles 12	1 Chronicles 13-29
John 1-4	John 5-7	John 8-10

Week 22	Week 23	Week 24
2 Chronicles 1-21	2 Chronicles 22-36	Ezra 1-Nehemiah 13
John 11-13	John 14-19	John 20-Acts 5

Week 25	Week 26	Week 27
Esther 1-Job 5	Job 6-23	Job 24-Job 40
Acts 6-9	Acts 10-13	Acts 14-17

Week 28 Job 41-Psalm 17 Acts 18-21	Week 29 Psalm 18-31 Acts 22-26	Week 30 Psalm 32-50 Acts 27-Romans 4
Week 31 Psalm 51-68 Romans 5-9	Week 32 Psalm 69-85 Romans 10-14	Week 33 Psalm 86-105 Romans 15-1 Corinthians 3
Week 34 Psalm 106-124 1 Corinthians 4-10	Week 35 Psalm 125-145 1 Corinthians 11-14	Week 36 Psalm 146-Proverbs 9 1 Cor 15-2 Cor 2
Week 37 Proverbs 10-23 2 Corinthians 3-10	Week 38 Proverbs 24-Ecclesiastes 8 2 Corinthians 11-Galatians 3	Week 39 Ecclesiastes 9-Isaiah 7 Galatians 4-Ephesians 4
Week 40 Isaiah 8-26 Ephesians 5-Colossians 1	Week 41 Isaiah 27-45 Colossians 2-1 Thessalonians 5	Week 42 Isaiah 46-66 2 Thessalonians 1-1 Timothy 6
Week 43 Jeremiah 1-15 2 Timothy 1-Titus 3	Week 44 Jeremiah 16-36 Philemon-Hebrews 6	Week 45 Jeremiah 37-52 Hebrews 7-11
Week 46 Lamentations 1- Ezekiel 16 Hebrews 12-James 3	Week 47 Ezekiel 17-33 James 4-1 Peter 5	Week 48 Ezekiel 34-48 2 Peter 1-1 John 5
Week 49 Daniel 1-Hosea 3 2 John-Jude	Week 50 Hosea 4-Amos 9 Revelation 1-10	Week 51 Obadiah-Zephaniah 3 Revelation 11-18
Week 52 Haggai 1-Malachi 4 Revelation 19-22		